MW01093837

UN-CRAP YOUR LIFE

UN-CRAP YOUR LIFE

Navigating Life's Crappiest Situations

STELLABELLE

Copyright © 2015 Stellabelle. All Rights Reserved.

DEDICATION

I dedicate this book to James Altucher.

*I discovered James Altucher's writing at a time when
my life was imploding in all directions. I was broke,
depressed, confused about how to make money from
my creativity and in a daily state of panic about
being a single mother. I was desperate for all kinds of
answers.*

I consumed James Altucher's writing like it was crack cocaine. I was hooked from the first blog post. His heartbreaking stories had an intense effect upon me. He exposed his failures and embarrassing thoughts in excruciating, raw detail and this created in me an instant feeling of trust.

He taught me to express my authentic voice and devise concrete ways to create income from my creativity. The most important lesson I learned from James is this: I cannot wait for someone to bestow power or importance upon me. I have to choose myself.

Unlike most superstars who make it, James Altucher continues to sincerely help those trapped in miserable situations. His empathy did not disappear with his rise to fame. This, above all else, is why I continue to read his books and be deeply influenced by him.

I hope I can be as honest as him one day.

CONTENTS

INTRODUCTION

I started writing this book in earnest six months ago when I received the news from an HR manager at a really good company:

"We're sorry, but you're not the right fit for us."

I asked the HR manager why I wasn't chosen. I explained I had been interviewed five different times and reminded her that one of her employees had referred me to her company. All I wanted to know was what characteristic prevented me from getting hired so in the future I could correct this defect. I begged her to tell me why. I was tired of not being chosen for good-paying jobs and was eager to fix myself.

She told me she honestly didn't know why I wasn't chosen. She said my skill set and work experiences were outstanding. At the end of our conversation, she confessed that the young, twenty-something hiring manager often made foolish decisions. The HR manager apologized numerous times and seemed honestly embarrassed I'd wasted so much of my time interviewing at her company.

After I got off the phone, failure and shame took turns ransacking my internal organs. My head filled with heat and my heart pumped uncontrollably. Then the nasty thoughts crept into my brain:

"I was rejected for being *me*. That hiring manager didn't like something about *me* and now I'm being punished. What the hell is wrong with *me*? Am I really a loser? Am I destined to have crappy jobs? Do I have a big letter "*L*" for "*Loser*" imprinted on my forehead that everyone else can see?"

Right after the feelings of failure and shame had washed over my body, I experienced a series of racing, flashing thoughts:

"I'm not sure I really wanted that job. I'm hurt not because I truly wanted it, but because I felt I was rejected as a person. Maybe instead of trying to find another job I'll most likely grow to dislike, I should write and self-publish a book? I've been writing for three years, so perhaps it's time to buckle down. Maybe it's time to test out my ideas and go all in. Maybe it's the day I make and keep a commitment to myself. Maybe it's the first day of un-crapping the rest of my life. I believe I'm in!"

I decided I would never again let another random person define my self-worth. From that day on, I decided to un-crap one thing about my life at a time. I decided to go all in. The very first thing I decided to un-crap was my inability to finish personal projects. I made a commitment to myself to finish this book in 2015. I decided not to let my perfectionism, inability to focus, lack of money, low self-esteem or my bad writing get in the way of this commitment. I pushed through every negative thought I had about myself in order to keep my commitment. My message to you is to make one commitment to yourself. Just one.

Once I made up my mind to self-publish a book, the next step was to decide on a topic. Many experts advise authors to write about topics they know really well. I asked myself, "What topic am I an expert on?" I thought about this for a long time. I scanned my life experiences and determined that above all, I'm a master at escaping from crappy situations. I'm good at recognizing bad situations and equally skilled when it comes to devising escape plans. My hope in writing this book is to help you escape from your own miserable situations, too. Each chapter ends with a list of exercises which are designed to get you thinking about possible solutions for your crappy life situations.

The time to un-crap your life is today. If you don't, you might find yourself near the end of your existence asking this question,

"Why didn't I go all in and create a life I wanted to live?"

I'm plagued by this thought in the middle of the night. It's high time to un-crap.

Are you ready? I am.

As I continue learning new ways to un-crap life, I'm happy to share them with you. Below is a link where you can sign up for my email newsletter.

http://leahstephens.weebly.com/sign-up-for-my-newsletter.html

I will never spam or sell your email address. I'll send you a newsletter only when I have something of value to say.

I look forward to learning from your reviews, emails and comments.

Just by reading this, you have helped me un-crap my life a little more.

Thank you so much.

Stellabelle

1

ARE YOU STUCK IN A CRAPTRAP?

Are you currently stuck in a craptrap?

Here are some signs you're stuck:

You let other people decide the course of your life.
You hate your job.
You hate your boss.
You frequently daydream while at your job and have trouble focusing on your work.
You wish you were doing something meaningful with your life instead of the 9-5.
You feel like you have a giant letter 'L' for 'Loser' imprinted on your forehead.
You're living paycheck to paycheck.
You drink or smoke to control your moods.
You go on Facebook in order to feel alive.
You drink to escape your life.
You check your smartphone notifications every two minutes.

You think someone is going to discover your talent or save you.
You're angry at the world because you feel cursed.
You feel you're too old and worn-out to change.
You feel no one truly understands you.
You have lost your ability to finish a personal project.
You're aware of your issues but feel unable to change them in any way.
When you get up in the morning, you're filled with unspeakable dread.
When you try to breathe, fear fills your lungs instead of oxygen and you only take shallow half-breaths.
When you remember the person you were in the past, you feel disconnected from him/her.
You cannot remember your childhood dreams.
Your goals seem like distant memories.
Your energies are being sucked into other people's dreams and your own dreams are withering in a corner.
You feel exhausted, powerless and hopeless.
You're afraid to stand up for yourself at work or home.
Your energies are scattered in too many directions.
You're just going through the motions in life and have lost passion.
You're frequently paralyzed by fear.
You're afraid of going broke.
When you think about your future, you visualize a vast gray field full of flightless, colorless birds who have lost their voices.

I have been all of these at different times in my life.

Every day I look for people who have made it out of their craptraps and I try to emulate them. The next step is to paint a picture of life outside your craptrap. I know what my life would be like without my traps because I lived without them for eight months in 2009. I explain what this felt like in the chapter, "I HATED LIVING IN KANSAS."

Confidence and self-esteem are essential components of dismantling your craptraps. But don't worry if your self-esteem is torn up, lying in a sad heap on the floor. It's still there, waiting for you to patch it together. I decided to write this book not because my self-esteem is at an all-time high, but because I'm slowly building it up. I'm embracing the slow building process instead of running away from it.

Without looking deeper into why you allowed your crappy situation to go on so long, you'll probably find yourself moving from one craptrap to the next. That's what I have done in the past. You'll never improve your life if you don't look deep inside and find the reasons why you continue live inside your craptraps. We've all been in a relationship that should have ended years before it actually did. Life situations are the same. Being able to identify your craptrap is the first step in getting out of it.

EXERCISES

What part of your life gives your the most worry?
When you go to sleep at night, what thoughts are racing through your mind?
What would other people say your craptrap is?
Can you remember a day when you were not in a craptrap?
If you can remember that day, what is different now?
Take Action: Write down on a piece of paper, MY CURRENT CRAPTRAP IS _____.

2

I WENT ON A DATE WITH A SERIAL KILLER

Ten years ago I saved my own life. At the time I worked at Barnes and Noble in the music department. I didn't enjoy being paid $8.50 an hour, but there were tons of jobs which were much worse. I frequently closed the store, which meant that I left work around 11:30 p.m. I had a lot of creepy experiences there including being stalked by a young guy named "Cornrows" and I endured antics from nut jobs who visited my department regularly. I'll never forget this one lunatic who showed up with black and purple makeup rings around his eyes. He came up to the counter to pay for a CD. After I told him the amount, he opened his billfold. He looked me dead in the eyes and said, "Go ahead, take it. Don't be scared." I looked at the bill. It was covered in dried blood.

Back then I did really stupid and thoughtless things. I was really into taking risks. I had low self-esteem and was naive. One night a tall, blonde, clean-cut, drop-dead gorgeous 20-something guy came to the music department. I was bored and struck up a conversation with him. He seemed pretty normal, low-key and looked a lot like Dolph Lundgren. I suggested we go get coffee after work and he agreed.

I met him outside the store and he had a duffel bag with him. I asked what was in it and he showed me several changes of clothes, all of which were sparkling clean. We talked about mundane topics until he sat down in my car. The second our car doors shut, he began telling me a super disturbing story of how his sister had raped him with a hot dog when he was 8 years old. He continued talking about inappropriate things, like how just two nights before he had slept with two different women at the same time. He followed this up with detailing how he had found a man doing karate in his backyard. He explained to me how he'd put his hands around the guy's neck and squeezed the last breath out of him. He showed no emotion while talking about last night's murder and he didn't care at all how his story was affecting me.

At this point, fear gripped my mind and it was clear I really screwed up by going on a date with this psycho. Would I be killed, raped, mutilated? Probably. A thousand ways to die flashed before me. I had to think of a way to get out of this fast. I settled on a plan quickly and decided to speak up. I said, "Hey, you're really freaking me out. No, you're scaring the shit out of me. Why would you do that? I wonder how your back would look if I clawed it with my nails until it bled? I wonder who will end up raping whom? I could rape you this instant. Then you'd be as afraid of me as I am of you right now."

He stopped talking and looked at me. I had no idea how he was going to react, but I succeeded in taking control of the conversation. We then talked feverishly about all sorts of strange and savage topics which I cannot recall. I would give anything to have recorded that conversation. I remember it being completely bizarre. When we reached the coffeehouse, I looked at him squarely and gave him a directive, "You are going to get out of my car now. We're not getting coffee. This is where it ends. I can't help you with your mountain of problems. You really need someone else, like a professional." He looked at me as he grabbed his duffel bag and replied, "You know, I usually get my way and do exactly what I want. I think this time I'll just let it go."

The look in his eyes was super disturbing. I saw death and murder in them. I could tell he meant what he said. I am lucky to be alive to tell this story.

SOLUTION: I SAVED MY LIFE BY TAKING CONTROL OF THE SITUATION

I have no evidence that he was a serial killer but he was either that or a sociopath. In either case, he was someone who did not respect me as a human being and who was not interested in my well being. This experience could have turned out horrifically if I had not paid attention to my gut instincts and taken control of the situation.

Looking back on this experience, it's clear I saved my own life. In the beginning of the car ride I noticed adrenalin flooded my body and my heart was racing uncontrollably. I paid close attention to these signals which alerted me to danger. Gut instincts are there for a reason. Pay close attention to them!

Then, I spent a fair amount of time listening to him. I asked probing questions to understand his fears, desires, weaknesses, psychology, strengths and current emotional state. After listening to him, I carefully analyzed his responses. I came to the conclusion he lacked empathy. I reached this conclusion because when he told me his story of being raped as a child, he wasn't interested in my reaction. He never looked over at me to gauge my response. As he continued on, he divulged more gruesome details while he stared off into space. He was just using me as his tool. Also, we were strangers and what kind of person tells such intimate details to a stranger? Only psychos do. These realizations scared me. It was the first indicator I was dealing with a sociopath or a killer.

The next thing I had to do was calm down so I could formulate an escape plan. I decided in order to take control of the situation I would first admit his stories were making me scared. When I confessed my feelings of fear, he snapped back to reality, stopped talking and just looked at me. This was the first time he reacted to me. Once I admitted my feelings of fear, I began to realize I could survive this encounter.

This little success gave me confidence to try another method of taking control: the crazy talk. I decided I would get on his level of insanity and see if I could take full control of the conversation. I did what he did to me: I scared him. I mirrored his personality. It worked. As my confidence grew, I decided the time had come to get him out of my car. When I gave him the directive to get out, I delivered this in an authoritative tone. Also, before I told him to get out, I explained I would be of no use to him in resolving the deep psychological wounds of his tortured past. I told him he should seek professional help. This method helped to focus the psycho on his own problems and away from me. When it came time for me to tell him to get out of my car, it was easy because I had been laying the groundwork of control for some time.

Actions arise from power dynamics. It is absolutely essential you create a plan to take control of your situation. It starts with your ability to assess the psycho and ends with you following through with your plan of escape. Remember all people have weaknesses, even those who are completely insane.

This experience also taught me people are not what they appear to be. I was really naive about people before this experience. I wish I could say it taught me a lesson and I never trusted a stranger again. My life was about to get really bad before I learned that lesson. I never saw this guy again and I never learned if he really was a serial killer. One thing I'm sure of: he was clearly insane.

EXERCISES

What is your gut telling you?

Are you paying close attention to your emotional reactions?

Ask the psycho probing questions to understand his weaknesses.

Ask questions to assess whether the psycho feels empathy or not.

Calm your mind before creating an escape plan.

Experiment with conversational topics and repeat whatever gives you the most control.

Take Action: Visualize yourself escaping from the psycho and create a plan.

3

I AM AN ADDICT

For much of my life drugs and alcohol have provided me with shortcuts to good moods. Achieving an amazing life goal takes years of hard, focused energy. With drugs, the good feelings arrive instantly. I've become addicted to almost everything I've ever tried. That's why I never tried heroin, meth or other nasty drugs. I knew they would eventually kill me.

In my teens, when I was a high fashion model, I was bulimic. Later, I became an alcoholic, got addicted to cigarettes, marijuana, and then much later, I became a fantasy addict. Fantasy addiction is a kind of love addiction. I became obsessed with people who didn't like me and who would never want me in a sexual way. I wanted to find out if I could ever get that person to sleep with me, to want me. Deep down I knew it wasn't possible. I chose unavailable men over and over again in order to avoid the deep pain that comes with all intimate relationships. This topic is really extensive and I wrote about one of my sexual obsessions in a blog post titled, *I'm Sorry You Were The Object of My Crazy Sexual Obsession.*

Alcohol was my primary addiction. I was in love with the feeling of being drunk. I drank on and off for about 18 years. Drinking alcohol worked so well that I became dependent on it in no time to solve my dark moods, social anxiety, lack of confidence and desire for creative adventure. Alcohol seemed to solve so many of my problems at once, I couldn't imagine a future without it. I used to proclaim during my drunken episodes, "I am made for drinking! Drinking is made for me! I will never be without it for it dances happily through my veins!" Everything was artificially wonderful until the next morning. Horrible doesn't even come close to describing my hangovers. I usually wanted to peel my skin off and jump into the abyss after a night of heavy drinking. Blackouts became a normal part of my drinking cycle.

In social situations, my anxiety dissolved a little more with each drink. My sober self was insecure and self-deprecating but my drunk self was confident and cocky. I went from pathetic to über confident after consuming three drinks. I suddenly felt attractive, fascinating and witty. One time a friend and I were at a party and an average-looking woman in a red dress walked by us. I was getting pretty drunk by this point and said to my friend, "I look better than *that.*" She burst out laughing. I would never say such a thing when I was sober. I liked the way alcohol cut through all the self-censoring bullshit inside my brain and extracted the horrible, raw truth. Alcohol brought my base desires to the surface and allowed me to act them out without judgement. The judgement, however, came hundredfold the next morning in the form of dark guilt.

I still remember those toxic feelings of guilt and how badly I wanted to escape their vise-like grip on my brain. An experience of dark guilt went something like this: first, a recollection of my bad drunken behavior from the night before would enter my consciousness. A rush of bad feelings would flood my body right after the recollection appeared in my mind. Then a stream of horrible things I regretted flowed past my brain: not sending a birthday card to my Mom five years ago, acting like an ass in public, not remembering to call someone back, etc. The thoughts were brought on by the toxic wasteland of an alcohol-saturated then alcohol-deprived brain. These dark guilt feelings then became the fuel for my next drinking binge. I wanted to escape these toxic feelings as soon as possible. This was the drinking cycle that controlled my brain for many years.

In 2006, I had a horrifying experience that woke up my mind to the realization I had a big problem with drinking. This episode happened after I had won an all-expenses paid trip to Los Angeles. Taschen Publishing had created an international online contest called Schlaupelz. There were ten collages with each one containing ten different partial images. Each image came from a different Taschen book cover, and whoever correctly identified the author and title of all 100 images won the contest. I spent a solid three months working on this contest so it's not surprising I won. Every person I mentioned this contest to told me I was silly for thinking I had a chance at winning. I didn't listen to anyone. I just continued to work on it every day after getting home from work.

My winning prize was an all-expenses paid trip to Los Angeles for two and I got to meet two Taschen writers of my choice. I chose Sven Kirsten and Dian Hanson. Sven is a German cinematographer who wrote *The Book of Tiki* and is based in Los Angeles. Dian writes or edits all the sexually explicit books for Taschen and one of her most recent titles at the time was *The Big Penis Book*.

After a thrilling day of meeting with the Taschen writers and going on a sightseeing trip with the head editor of Taschen, I felt over-stimulated and ready for more. I didn't want the excitement to end and suggested to my friend that we have some drinks at the hotel bar. She didn't want to do that. She decided to retire for the evening. I wanted to celebrate my amazing win and take it further. I decided to go to the hotel bar by myself and have a few celebratory drinks.....or ten.

After having three gin and tonics, I met two brothers at the hotel bar. One of them had long curly brown hair and was a bit revolting physically. I remember thinking I would never be interested in him if I was sober. I don't remember too many details about them but we all decided to go to their room after drinking heavily at the bar. I made out with both of them and I have only sketchy memories of what took place, but I do remember they helped me back to my room. I woke up the next morning with gigantic, watermelon-sized bruises on my hip and chest. I had no memory of how I got them and it scared the crap out of me. I thought I must have fallen down, but I wasn't sure and the not being sure part is what scared me the most. The day I found those gigantic bruises was the day I realized I had some big problems to solve. I could have easily been murdered by those brothers since they were complete strangers.

I tried to stop drinking after this episode but my brain had become dependent upon alcohol by this point.

Then in 2009, my body had had enough of processing alcohol. I would frequently get sick the next day after drinking only a little and it was obvious I needed to stop. After seeing a shrink, I was given Paxil. This drug worked really well and I quit smoking and drinking without even trying. It had other strange side effects, but that's another story. Even before taking Paxil I had begun to replace some of my addictive behaviors with creating art. I knew it was time for my drinking to end if I was going to live.

SOLUTION: I OVERCAME A LOT OF MY ADDICTIONS BY SEEKING HELP AND FINDING TRUE SOURCES OF HAPPINESS

Here's how I began the process of healing myself from my alcohol addiction: I sought help from a medical professional, wrote down things from my childhood that made me happy and explored the activities which used to bring me true joy. This exercise helped me understand I love to learn new things and experiment. I learned I'm happiest when I'm in control of my life. I learned above all, I enjoy seeing my creative ideas come to life. The act of creating is essential to my well-being. I value imagination over everything else. I also learned I'm very happy when I have helped someone discover their true passions, dormant within them for years.

I used alcohol primarily to control my moods. Now when I start to feel anxious, I don't try to immediately alter my feelings. First, I analyze what sources are creating the anxiety. Some anxiety I experience is necessary for survival. For example, I feel anxious about my job since I know deep down, I don't like my current one and have no interest in it. I want to be putting my energies into work I believe in and which also brings me monetary stability. I know the anxiety I feel is propelling me towards a life which is more meaningful.

Then there is the anxiety which stems from my past experiences with an abusive ex-boyfriend. This anxiety is much harder to deal with. Instead of turning to drugs or alcohol to diminish my anxiety, I'm learning how to first acknowledge the pain and then become more detached from it in order to heal. It goes like this in my head, "Oh, hello again Anxiety. I see you've returned. I understand you've taken over my body and emotions temporarily. I feel your presence. And now that I've said hello, I'm going to go over here and think a bit. I'm sure I'll see you again soon. I give you permission to leave. Goodbye for now. See you soon."

I also began to tell the truth. For most of my life I had been scared to tell people how I felt. I was afraid of conflict. I was afraid of letting them down. I thought if I let them down, they would not love me anymore. This was part of my programming. We all have been programmed in our lives and it is up to us as adults to discard the programs that no longer serve our growth. I realized in order for me to get better, I needed to start telling the truth to myself and others.

Other things I did: wrote about my experiences, shared them with others who have similar issues and most importantly, learned what I needed to do to make my brain feel good.

The last thing I did was allow myself to be assertive. I noticed when I drank I would become super obnoxious, loud, demanding, overly sexual and cocky. The alcohol allowed me to express parts of myself I did not accept. I had banished those parts of my personality to the cellar and now the alcohol had unlocked the door! My obnoxious and sexually aggressive traits were hissing, spitting and emerging like crazy, starved victims!

Being assertive was not part of who I perceived myself to be. My core personality was not aggressive as far as I knew. I viewed myself as a withdrawn, shy person. At least this is how people defined me as a young woman.

As I got older, however, a stronger, more forceful person developed inside. I drank in order to integrate this new trait into my existing personality. The way I was able to stop this vicious drinking cycle was to allow myself to be assertive when I was sober. I would say things exactly as they were. I didn't sugarcoat anything. I didn't lie to myself or others. It was really awkward at first. I said "No" to people for the first time in my adult life. And it worked. The more I unconditionally accepted that little obnoxious, opinionated monster within me, the less I needed to drink in order to bring it out. The more I let out my monster into the sunlight, the less angry it was. I became my drunk self while sober, to a certain extent.

I now allow myself to be as outspoken and honest as I want to be, as long as I don't hurt others. I am still learning how to be outspoken and polite at the same time. I'm not very good at it yet since it's a fairly new experience.

I'm currently not taking any medications and I no longer crave alcohol or any other drugs. I still have some issues with social media, but nothing else. This is a miracle since I thought I would be addicted to drinking forever. I mistakenly believed that my brain needed a substance to function well. I'm now learning techniques to access good feelings naturally by re-wiring my neural pathways. I'm also learning the importance of setting and attaining challenging goals. For further reading on how brain chemicals work, read *Meet Your Happy Chemicals* by Loretta Breuning. This book helped me understand how my brain works and what it needs to do in order to feel good.

While writing this book, I stumbled upon a *Huffington Post* article by Johann Hari in which he asserts that "addiction is an adaptation. It's not you. It's your cage." Here's the most startling information from Hari's post:

"But in the 1970s, a professor of Psychology in Vancouver called Bruce Alexander noticed something odd about this experiment. The rat is put in the cage all alone. It has nothing to do but take the drugs. What would happen, he wondered, if we tried this differently? So Professor Alexander built Rat Park. It is a lush cage where the rats would have colored balls and the best rat-food and tunnels to scamper down and plenty of friends: everything a rat about town could want. What, Alexander wanted to know, will happen then?

In Rat Park, all the rats obviously tried both water bottles, because they didn't know what was in them. But what happened next was startling.

The rats with good lives didn't like the drugged water. They mostly shunned it, consuming less than a quarter of the drugs the isolated rats used. None of them died. While all the rats who were alone and unhappy became heavy users, none of the rats who had a happy environment did."

This theory is an interesting way to think about addiction. During some of my periods of heavy drinking, I was definitely alone in a cage and sought ways to get out of it. During most of my adult years I did not have long-term relationships and was generally afraid of intimacy. This trait I think made me more susceptible to turning to substances to feel good and to connect to others.

We need to rethink what addiction means. It's not useful to think about quitting a drug. Quitting never worked for me. What worked for me was replacing my addiction to alcohol with something else. In the very beginning, an antidepressant medication called Paxil replaced alcohol. Then later, I began to discover other activities that created immensely happy brain chemicals: writing, getting therapy, making art, reading, making friends with people I admired, designing a life instead of living the 9–5, and taking on big life challenges. And I still continue the method of constant replacement to this day.

I created some videos to explore the topic of overcoming alcohol addiction. It's in a folder called *Addictions* on my YouTube channel, **Stellabelle**. The videos in this folder explore alcoholism in-depth and provide detailed analyses of the reasons I used to drink. I named them, "How To Overcome Alcoholism Without Joining AA." I have nothing against AA but I couldn't never quite embrace the idea of a higher power. Woo woo stuff makes me cringe and I prefer to study life problems by digging until I discover the root causes of pain. It's my belief that our inability to reach our dreams in adulthood stem from an issue that was never properly dealt with, acknowledged or managed in an earlier part of life.

If you're an addict, what explanations resonate with you?

EXERCISES:

Ask yourself what problem(s) drugs or drinking solves for you.
Write down what you liked to do as a child.
What is one activity that makes you feel really good (besides your addiction).
Write down a dream you let die.
Write down a personality trait you don't accept about yourself.
Write down a personality trait that emerged later in life.
Write down something you want to achieve before you die.
Write down something you do while drunk that you wouldn't do sober.
Take Action: Film yourself drunk. Watch it. Take notes.

4

I HATED LIVING IN KANSAS

I had grown tired of living in Kansas in 2006. It felt boring. I was done with cornfields. I wanted the beach, sand and sun. I wanted to live among the palm trees and meet fascinating people who were really laid back or a little crazy. I wanted to swim with dolphins and fish. I wanted to meet rebels who lived life differently. I wanted to move to California. I didn't have a job there and didn't know anyone who lived in California. But I had two things: $2000 and determination.

There was another reason I wanted to move to California: my drunken sexual escapades had gotten out of control. I was having blackouts during my binge drinking nights and I couldn't remember what I had done and with whom. I would occasionally run into someone with whom I slept or someone I had pissed off during one of my escapades. I had no clue what I had done because I couldn't piece together my drunken memories. It had gotten really uncomfortable to face the horrible person I had become. I longed to live in a place that hadn't been tainted with my drunken insanity.

SOLUTION: I SOLD OR GAVE AWAY MOST OF MY STUFF AND MOVED TO CALIFORNIA AT AGE 36 WITH $2000

The two things standing in my way were: finding a job in my chosen city and getting rid of most of my material things. I felt material possessions were a hindrance to my plan of moving to a new city. So I sold my entire cd and record collection to a music store, gave away most of my art and furniture to thrift stores, then dropped off my life-sized rotating Chinese dolls at a friend's house. I bought two weeks' worth of summer clothes and got rid of the rest of my wardrobe. I only kept what would fit in my car.

The first step in this process is to figure out where you want to live. If you already know where you want to live, the next thing you need to do is secure a job there. The job market was different in 2006, so what worked then may not work today. However, I do have a few tips to help you find employment in a different city. In 2006 when I moved to San Diego, I used Craigslist to find a job doing graphic art. In my resume, I used a San Diego address of a youth hostel where I stayed previously. When the prospective employer called me, I acted as if I lived in San Diego. In my mind, I had already moved there, so it was relatively easy for me to pretend I lived there. I think it would have been difficult to secure a job if I hadn't changed my resume in this way.

Once I arrived in San Diego, I stayed at a $20 per night youth hostel. You can stay at youth hostels even if you're not in your twenties. The next day I began scouring the apartment rental ads on the internet, in newspapers and on Craigslist. I found a room and board house which was fairly inexpensive. The operation was run by a businesswoman named Gabriel, and after meeting with her, I signed up immediately. Her house had a beautiful pool and a quiet feel to it. My gut instincts were positively aligned with a yes.

The job I had secured in San Diego was working as a colorist for an eccentric, talentless millionaire. He was the son of a real estate baron and fancied himself a genius artist and musician. He hired me to color in the pages of a comic book he had produced. He wasn't talented enough to create the artwork himself, but he had money to hire an army of creative people to do art he envisioned. The comic book I worked on wasn't especially bad but it wasn't good, either. On my first day on the job at his mansion, I thought I was the luckiest person alive since I was allowed to take swimming breaks in his private pool. Also, his place was filled with surreal stuff: a mouth-shaped chair, bamboo doors, psychedelic couches and colorful odd costumes.

Things went downhill very quickly. He couldn't remember the password to get into the computer assigned to me. He became violently angry and blamed the other artists for this.

After he finally found the password, I started coloring in parts of the comic book. He stood right behind me and dictated the shade of red I should use to color in the heroine's lips. I thought he would go away after a while and let me do the work by myself, but he didn't. He wanted to tell me the exact colors to use for each section, each page. It was insane. Micromanagement is one thing I cannot tolerate at all. Then the next day, during a lunch break, he put his hands down his pants to scratch his balls. I was done. I lasted two days.

I began job-hunting the very next day. I found a decent job in La Jolla working at a print shop. It's important to always be moving, looking and searching for opportunities when you're living in a new place. Don't let bad situations get you down. View everything as an experiment. Some experiments will fail while others will succeed. I viewed my experience with the talentless millionaire as a stepping stone to moving to San Diego. I paid attention to my gut instincts and moved on to better things when situations got too weird. You can do this, too.

My tendency to be self-reliant coupled with an adventure-seeking personality were key components in my ability to pick up and move to a new city at age 36 with only $2000 in my pocket. My parents had taken my brother and I to Europe several times when I was young. They instilled in us a love of travel.

I traveled by myself extensively in Chicago and Tokyo when I was in my teens and twenties. I had developed street smarts, confidence and a lack of fear with regard to new experiences. The development of these traits was the reason I found success in San Diego in such a short time. If you're thinking of doing something similar, I would recommend you first go on a small trip by yourself and see how you like it. Moving to a new place can be difficult if you're not self-reliant.

The best thing to do for yourself when you move to a new city is to remember you are ultimately in control. If your gut is telling you something doesn't feel right, get out of the situation. I've saved my own life countless times by paying really close attention to my instincts.

For example, one night I was driving myself home from a bar at 2 A.M. I was on a one-way street, at a stop light. A car came up behind me. A man got out of his car and started running towards mine. I reacted with lightning speed, slammed the gas pedal to the floor and drove away, through a red light. I had already scanned for oncoming cars, so going through the red light was safe. There was no logical reason why the guy would do this because his car was running. I made a split second decision based on my survival instinct. You can do this, too.

EXERCISES:

Are you craving a new adventure in a new place?
If you want to move, what are the obstacles in your way?
If material possessions are in your way, could you give away or sell most of your stuff?
If you could live anywhere where would it be?
Have you traveled alone before?

If you want to move, what are you most afraid of?

Take Action: If you want to move somewhere new, make an action plan to do it.

5

THE 2008 RECESSION KILLED MY JOB

The year was 2008 and the recession was making my company go downhill fast. My 401K plan had lost more than $2,000 and the vice president had just walked out. Work that used to take me eight hours to complete, I was getting done in four. Our customers were disappearing and I felt like I was on the Titanic. The feeling of powerlessness was everywhere. I decided something drastic was necessary but I was not sure what to do. I knew if I stayed at my job I would most likely be laid off. Quitting seemed like suicide in such a volatile time. After thinking about the possibilities for about two weeks, I decided that I would begin to search for a new job.

I went to a restaurant to interview for a designer position and the entire place was filled with applicants. It was a humiliating experience. The next day I answered an ad for a cashier position at Trader Joe's. Six hundred people showed up and I was told to leave. After these two experiences I gave up. I knew there was something bigger going on with the economy. There were few jobs in Southern California in 2008 and I decided not to waste any more time applying for jobs I wouldn't get. I opted to take a completely different and riskier route.

SOLUTION: I CASHED OUT MY 401K, TAUGHT MYSELF NEW SKILLS AND MET INSPIRING PEOPLE

I decided I would spend my time learning things I never had time for when I was employed. I had always wanted to learn how to compose music on my computer. I also wanted to learn how to make a YouTube channel. I wanted to paint my car and become a street performer. There were tons of things I wanted to do, so I decided to learn and do as much as I could until my money ran out. I wasn't even sure how long that would be. I had about $8,000 in my 401K and very few monthly expenses.

One of the first things I did was cover my walls with giant pieces of butcher paper. Then I wrote down my desired goals on the sheets of paper. I had tons of goals and things I wanted to do. Once I finished the goals on one piece of paper, I'd write down an entire column of new ideas on a new sheet of paper. Once I achieved my goals, I'd cross them off. This method allowed me to constantly be aware of both what I still wanted to accomplish and what I had already done. Once I filled up an entire wall, I'd start the process again. I got an enormous amount of goals achieved this way.

Through this process, I became keenly aware of my creative thoughts and inner world. I began having artistic visions and I experienced life in a magical fashion. I met amazing people with great ease and was delighted to learn new things. I was excited to be alive.

One of my experiments involved creating a persona called the *Patron Saint of Postcards*. The creation of this came to me in a vision. People are always misunderstanding the word *vision*. For me, having a vision means an idea emerges from the deep well of my imagination and presents itself to my conscious mind. Dreams are unconscious visions. The reason I could nurture and grow these visions is I didn't have to be at a job every day. I would never had these visions come to life if I had been working a 9-5 job.

The *Patron Saint of Postcards* experiment was like performance art and busking mixed together. I had a costume built and I created about 100 handmade postcards, which I carried in a bright green custom-made apron. I would then sell or give away my postcards to people I randomly met. The main reasons I did this were to experiment with human behavior, create side income and share my postcard art with the public directly. I recorded a lot of material from this experiment and you can see it on my YouTube channel, **Stellabelle**, in a folder named, *Patron Saint of Postcards.*

This experiment also created a new type of commerce. The price of the postcard would depend on the type of interaction I had with each person. If a person was genuinely interested and excited about my postcards, they would get them for free. Conversely, if a person asked what the price was and just seemed interested in purchasing them, they paid $4 per postcard. This experiment proved very successful in creating thought-provoking exchanges. The best reaction I ever received was from a 12-year-old boy at a festival in Carlsbad, California. I walked by this boy then he stopped in front of me. He waved his hands in front of his face quickly, looked up at me in disbelief and said, "Are you real?" I just shook my head and said, "No." I could tell he was convinced he was seeing something from his imagination. Through this experimental phase I learned most people are not accustomed to seeing costumes which people make up from their own creativity. The vast majority of costumes we are exposed to are copies of Hollywood characters or historical personas. I've been creating my own characters and costumes since childhood so it feels just like a normal part of life.

While I was experiencing life as the *Patron Saint of Postcards* and living out my creative fantasies, my life began to morph into a dynamic artistic adventure. I started meeting fascinating people and being accepted into elite groups of artists. I met great artists like Alex Chiu and Neil Mclean, who greatly influenced my direction. Alex Chiu at the time was a prolific comic artist. His art possesses a psychedelic feel coupled with a unique sense of humor.

I met Neil Mclean through a mutual friend, when he worked as a music video and stop motion animation film director. His music videos included work for Saything, Ladytron, The Coral, Pop Levi and others. His current project is *Dungeon,* an amazing and intricate sci-fi stop motion animated film. After seeing the preview for *Dungeon,* I wrote to Neil and told him how much I loved his work.

Here's my email to Neil:

> "Your Dungeon preview was remarkable and made me splatter giggles all over Caldwell's antique store. I think the giggles are still there, in faint forms, quivering in between dusty books, or something like that. I especially liked the names of the characters and your voice which sounded utterly ridiculous. The other things I liked are too numerous to list, so let's just say that you definitely have a fan, and I would pay sums of money to see it on the big screen. Are you going to show it locally when you finish it?"

After he received my email, he asked if I would be available to play a role in *Dungeon.* Here is my response to him:

> "Of course I would stand in for Kate!!!! Are you insane????? I would cut off my own toenail, double-bake it, add bits of my own crispy-fried hair, put it into a cocktail glass and use my pet squirrel's moustache as a decorative umbrella and drink it in one gulp to be part of DUNGEON!!!!"

Having been given the opportunity to work with Neil on *Dungeon* was one of the highest points in my life. I learned the world will open up once you reveal what you truly love and admire. For most of my life I had remained secretive about what I admired and truly loved. I wanted to protect my vulnerable feelings of admiration. This experience taught me that people, no matter how famous or brilliant, still have the same basic human needs the rest of us do. We all need feedback and validation that our work is having a positive effect on others.

I experienced my happiest moments in the company of these creators. They reinforced the idea that imagination is the most important aspect of being alive. This notion was something I believed in, but before I met them, I did not know many who believed like me.

I ended up in the *San Diego CityBeat* newspaper several times for my antics as the *Patron Saint of Postcards*. I met one of the *CityBeat* writers one night while I was showing my postcards to several people at a bar. This writer was instantly intrigued by my odd persona and life stories and he completed an interview with me on the spot. I felt like I was on the verge of getting famous. But it didn't exactly happen.

There was one big flaw in my plan: I didn't create a big enough income flow from my artistic activities. Making between $12 and $20 per day as The Patron Saint of Postcards didn't exactly cut it. This lack of foresight caused me to go broke. At this point in my life, however, I was not ready to launch any big financial master plan. I had no idea about income generation. I was in the beginning stages of exploring my passions, meeting inspiring people and having adventures.

The main outcomes of cashing out my 401K were the following:

- I was asked to do acting in Neil Mclean's stop motion animated film *Dungeon*.
- I learned how to compose music on my computer.
- I learned how to make YouTube videos.
- I got in fantastic physical condition.
- I lived out some creative fantasies including creating the persona, *The Patron Saint of Postcards*.
- I learned how to act on creative impulses without judging myself.

- I created a short film, called *Slab of Salvation*, about a visionary artist named Leonard Knight.

- I met inspiring people who changed my life forever: a Hollywood voice artist, a music video director, a toothpaste inventor, the owner of a psychedelic gift shop, a retired general manager of a car dealership who now calls himself Dolphin Boy, a self-help guru, a cartoonist, a street performer, a glass blower, a charismatic writer, an 87-year-old ex-alcoholic former millionaire salsa dancer.

The recession taught me to look within myself for answers. It taught me not depend on a company for all my needs. It taught me the world is in a constant state of change and I have to constantly change with it or perish. The days of being a lazy cubicle worker are finished. Looking back, I'm glad I had the nerve to cash out my 401K and live out my dreams, even if it only lasted eight months. The lessons I learned from this period will last forever. It was the most valuable plunge I've ever taken in my life. It also created the foundation for many of my future creative endeavors.

Cashing out a 401K is not recommended for people who are risk averse. In fact, this idea is not very practical in many ways. Before you do it, you have to figure out how much money you require to live on each month. And a smarter plan would be to create an income stream before you live off your retirement funds. But I do recommend cashing out a 401K for those who are sick of being corporate slaves and those who do not know what their passions are. Just make sure you have a support system in place before you jump off the cliff.

EXERCISES

If you work at a job, what are some things you don't have time to do?
Name one thing you would love to do if you had unlimited time and resources.

If you had an unlimited supply of courage, what would you attempt?
Who do you admire?
Do you have dreams of what you would like to try?
Take Action: Send an email or letter to someone you truly admire.

6

I SANK INTO SOUL-CRUSHING POVERTY

The year 2013 was hell for me. I was broke. What I mean by broke might have a different meaning from what you know. I was so devoid of money that the thought of buying a stick of deodorant for myself sent fear up my spine. I was on food stamps. I sold every last meaningful possession on eBay, including my GoPro camera, my vintage feather hat and a giant ink drawing I did in my late twenties. I sold my 16" x 20" drawing for $15 to some guy in New York. I loved the drawing and never intended to sell it. I had to sell it.

In my desperation I would frequently ask advice from my friends. It's important to ask for help when you need it and then take action when someone gives you good advice. That's what I did when I started working in car sales. It's scary to try new things, but in order to go forward, sometimes you have to jump off a cliff and see what happens.

SOLUTION: I GOT A JOB IN CAR SALES, FOUND SIDE JOBS, REDUCED EXPENSES AND SAVED UP $7000 IN TWO YEARS

One of my friends, who was previously the general manager of a car dealership, encouraged me to sell cars. He convinced me I would be good at it. After a year of indecision, I finally decided to try it out. I was hired at the first dealership I applied and began selling Toyotas in November of 2013. I was not wildly successful mainly because I'm not an aggressive person and I don't enjoy standing for hours doing nothing except staring out into a car lot waiting to pounce on a customer. I don't like it when sales people approach me either, but this is another story. In my year and a half at the dealership, I was able to make a decent income and put $7,000 into my savings account.

On my days off, I frequently earned income from focus groups. I did research to find the best company in Kansas City paying the most money for my opinions. I received between $75 and $200 for each focus group project. I've received money for taste tests and mock court cases. A greeting card company paid my daughter and I to find out which new toy products we liked the best.

You have to be persistent, though, because you won't qualify for all the focus groups. Also, my best advice to really poor people is this: when the survey asks for your income, put down $35,000 per year. That's what I did and I think it's okay to fudge the numbers because you're the one who needs the cash. The money I received from Q & A Focus Suites when I was flat broke was like heaven. Pursue this if you're desperate for cash.

I also earn money from my videos. I enter contests if there's a cash award. I also receive a small amount from Google for my YouTube videos. In all, I've probably made about $500 from Google, a few thousand from video contests, and a few more thousand making videos for people and companies. I recently won a $550 cash award for a video contest which my dealership sponsored.

I've learned from entrepreneurs it's really important to have many sources of income. It's my goal to have five different solid sources of income in the future.

My car was totalled last year and I was forced to buy one. I decided I wanted a low monthly payment. I drive a lot so I wanted either an electric or hybrid car. The Nissan Leaf's range wasn't good enough, so I decided to get a Prius. Since I worked at a car dealership I bought a Certified 2011 Prius for the invoice price. My monthly payment is $190 and my monthly fuel cost is $80. I saved money by paying for an oil change program in advance. Through my research I learned the Prius is a very reliable car. It has been so far. My dream car is a Tesla, so I most likely will not be driving the Prius when the hybrid battery needs to be replaced.

My daughter goes to a preschool at a cost of $680 per month. In 2013, when I was completely broke, my mother asked my brother if he could help pay for preschool expenses. He said yes and he has paid for several years. This expense will be ending in two months, so I will be saving that as well. My parents take care of my daughter when I am working late, which happens often. Without this help, my life would be pretty dismal.

I rarely buy new clothes for myself. I don't spend money on booze, movies, bars, concerts, events or other entertainment, as my life has changed dramatically. In my free time, I read, write, do social media, make art and videos, and spend time with my daughter and family. Time is my most precious commodity.

I cut my own hair and have done so since I was 18 years old. I've saved 27 years worth of haircuts. Over my lifetime, I calculate I've saved about $3,240 by cutting my own hair.

Eating out enhances the quality of my life. As a busy person, I rarely have time to cook. I allow myself to spend money eating out because it's the one luxury that improves my life. I used to feel guilty every time I spent money at a restaurant, but I've decided to embrace it now. I deny myself of so many other things that eating out is the one thing I feel good about, plus it solves many problems all at once, like food preparation, washing dishes and cleaning up the dinner table. I enjoy cooking but not on a regular basis. I like to experiment with food and create odd new concoctions like frozen grape milk, pickle pancakes and brain-shaped cake pops. I view food as both nourishment and artistic experimentation.

In 2013, my daughter and I were living in a room that cost $500 per month. This $500 included everything. I had no other housing expenses. I lived in a Hyde Park mansion with a family of 10. We had full access to the house, including the kitchen, yard, living rooms and pool. It was a positive experience, but after a while, I felt cramped and wanted my own space.

I began looking for houses. It was a scary thought considering I would be in debt for 25+ years. The idea of being tied to an expensive mortgage was too frightful. Then I had a dream. In the dream I was peering over my father's shoulder to see how much he had left to pay on his house. In the dream I could never determine how much he owed. When I woke up from the dream, I knew what course I should take. I should take over the mortgage, considering it would be a lot less than starting from the beginning of a mortgage. I found out that he owed $50,000 on the 5 bedroom house and his monthly mortgage payment is $450 per month. So, now I pay the $450 mortgage payment. When I pay off the $50,000 I will own the house. So now we all live together and my child care costs have evaporated with the move. My father frequently watches my daughter while I work late. We all split the costs for everything. We're also considering renting out one of the rooms on AirBnb to cover more expenses.

I have other random expenses. I buy my daughter new clothes and other things on special occasions, but I don't buy expensive gifts on a regular basis. I do buy expensive electronics when I need them, as I just purchased the iPhone 6 Plus and spent nearly $900. It is completely worth it. It's a great tool. Before I got the iPhone 6 Plus, I had a hand-me-down iPhone 4 from my brother. He's always getting the newest Apple stuff, so he'd give me his older electronics, including the MacBook I'm currently typing on.

Looking at this list it is apparent my family's help combined with not spending money on non-essential things are the two reasons I was able to save up $7,000. If I tried to do all this on my own and I spent a lot on myself, I probably wouldn't have a dime. As I create new forms of income, I will write about them. Stay tuned!

EXERCISES

If you need extra money have you considered doing market research projects?
Are there any bills you could get rid of, for example, switching from cable TV to 100% internet?
Do you have family members who can help you with childcare?
Is your job paying you adequately?
When is the last time you requested a raise?
Do you believe you can get out of poverty?
Take Action: Make a list of jobs that would get you out of poverty then start applying for them. If you want to start working for yourself, create a plan and start working on it every day.

7

MY VICIOUS CYCLE: BAD JOBS

I've had some really bad jobs: security guard, assistant lunch lady, temp worker, cook, factory worker, car saleswoman, photo printer, tile glazer, food runner, waitress and doggy daycare worker. I've had some good jobs also: graphic artist, English teacher and prepress technician. I reached the glass ceiling in my good jobs and wanted more income. I'm college-educated and fairly intelligent, but I lacked self-esteem and common sense sometimes. I moved around a lot so I had to re-establish connections each time I relocated. I've lived in Japan, Arizona, California, Kansas and Missouri.

I come from an upper middle-class background and I never put any serious thought into how to make money. When I was younger, I assumed it would just randomly appear in my bank account. I know this sounds ridiculous, but it's the truth. I certainly never learned anything money-related in college. I was too busy memorizing Japanese characters, creating fake art styles like *flour arté* and making odd films with my best friend.

There was no class called *What You Do For Money After You Graduate.*

After college, my friend and I moved to Tucson, Arizona on a whim. We never put much thought into how we were going to support ourselves once we got there. After looking through a few days' worth of want-ads, we found jobs at a faux Native American art factory.

My friend became a miniature art painter and I became a decorative tile glazer. It started off pretty good as I enjoyed learning the craft of tile glazing. I took pride in calling myself an artisan. But the bad things began piling up fairly quickly after I'd learned the basics of my job. I didn't much like the fact that the owners were white people who were ripping off the art and designs of Native Americans. The male owner who I'll now refer to as Lil' Asswipe, was verbally abusive to all his workers. My wages were so low that I was unable to buy food after the rent and utilities were paid. My rent was pretty low, so that did not account for my inability to buy food. The wages were the real problem.

Lil' Asswipe would often start off our day by screaming at us, "I don't want any sick babies tomorrow!" Most of the workers were women with children. He cracked sexist jokes. He defined the word scum.

The first time he screamed at us marked the beginning of my intense and imaginative revenge fantasies. I knew I wasn't going to let this bastard get away with treating us like worthless creatures. Every day I said under my breath, "Lil' Asswipe, you are going to pay dearly for abusing us. I don't know which day it will be, but it will come to pass."

My anger and hatred for this little man grew for months until I could no longer contain it. I had moved from the revenge fantasy stage into the revenge action stage. My first revenge plan was simple: I'd walk up to him and punch him in the face. But I didn't want to go to jail, so I crossed that one off. My second plan was to walk up to him while carrying a tray of freshly painted tiles and "accidentally" trip, thereby spilling the wet tiles onto his face. The hope would be either the glaze or the sharp edges of the tiles would do some bodily harm to him. I rehearsed this plan for days and days and was very close to enacting it. I felt a rush of dopamine every time I rehearsed it in my mind. I practiced what I would say, how I would trip, and what I would say afterwards. But in the end, I chickened out. I didn't want to go to jail and feared my plan would somehow backfire.

So, I created a third and final plan that I actually carried out. Here's how it went down: I told my best friend about it and she agreed to go along. On our final day, we painted and glazed all kinds of morbid creatures on our artwork instead of the Southwestern designs we were instructed to do. I painted dark ghosts, angry wolves and wide-eyed alien children onto my tiles all morning long.

After painting and glazing these bizarre figures for several hours, I decided the time was right to pay Lil' Asswipe a visit to his office. I calmly opened the door and locked eyes with him at the first opportunity. I began speaking, "Dear boss of mine, I'm so sad to leave this beautiful, fun place you've created for us slaves. Today is such a sad day for me. I'm sad too, as I will no longer be helping you and your dear wife build your mansions from the sweat off my back. I'm glad you two can enjoy your leisure time spent in luxurious surroundings while your workers are traveling to various food banks just so they don't starve to death. And your jokes, I'm going to miss those funny jokes! And I'll never forget your words, 'No sick babies'. I have a little question for you. Want to hear it? I thought you'd say yes. Do you know why I know how to make a killer bowl of ramen noodles? I didn't think you knew the answer. There's a lot you will never know. But, I'm not going to stick around any longer to enlighten you, you worthless piece of shit." After I said the word, *shit*, I could sense his shiftiness and fear. I decided this would be a good time to bolt out of his office. I didn't let him say one word. Not one. I was gone just as fast as I had zoomed in!

After I walked out, I had a rush. A serious rush! I was alive, happy and not in jail. I returned the horrors and insults to the person who had created them. I had spoken for everyone and I had spoken the truth. Later that same day, I found out that Lil' Asswipe had called my best friend into his office after I walked out. He asked her if I was organizing a worker's revolt. It was genius! I had put the fear into his blood and now he was scared that his workers were going to revolt against him! I, the little person I felt I was, had scared a bad grown man! My job was now complete. It was time to move on.

SOLUTION: REALIZED WHAT MY LIMITS WERE AND DESIGNED A PLAN FOR PAYING BILLS PLUS CREATING MY OWN INCOME

I'm not suggesting you do anything dangerous or criminal when you decide you've simply had enough of your own desperate job situation. I am suggesting, however, you begin to really listen to your own needs. If you suspect your boss might be an abusive, narcissistic shithead, he/she probably is. Your mind will create revenge scenarios for you if you decide to ignore your emotional life. When your work environment is abusive and you're a decent person, you will begin to internalize the abuse. Then the build-up of those negative feelings will most likely make you mentally or physically ill. This has happened many times in my working career.

So, it's necessary to create a plan relieving your mental tensions but doesn't land you in jail. When I left the Native American rip-off factory, I felt it was in my best interest to communicate to my evil boss just how horrible he was. I also felt it was important to at least try and improve a bad situation because hundreds of employees were still being treated badly. I thought if I tried to make my boss self-reflect, there would be a chance for change. The change might include a reduction in suffering on the part of the employees. I followed the direction of my conscience by confronting my boss directly and I allowed the possibility of change to occur. I never found out what happened, though.

The average workplace sucks. Everyone is afraid of getting fired. Disengagement happens frequently at corporate jobs. Most corporations are run like slave factories. Individuals are not valued for their unique gifts and are viewed as cheap, refillable lighters. When they are fired they are not even allowed to say goodbye to their coworkers. They are yelled at, dehumanized and told to get out. This is the current state of affairs at most modern companies. I just witnessed this at my last job. Low morale reigns supreme when an environment is super toxic. Of course there are some really good places to work, but not for the majority of people. After the recession, a lot of employees found themselves doing the work of two people for the same amount of money. Salaries have remained flat. Fear is the water that everyone is drinking at companies. It's not a pretty situation.

I've had lots of crappy jobs. The job I had until recently was crappy. I sold cars at a dealership.

The two main reasons it was crappy were: extreme micromanagement and disrespect of employees. If someone expressed an opinion which did not align with the opinion of the head boss, the employee was fired on the spot without any due process. The atmosphere was full of blame and suffocating levels of fear.

But I made a lot more money selling cars than at the job I had before. I used to live paycheck to paycheck. This was a bad deal because it didn't let me accumulate any money. I needed to have some money saved up when I decided to make the transition from working for others to working for myself. I think the transition would have been nearly impossible to do without having some financial cushion.

My job was far from ideal, but it enabled me to develop social skills and taught me a good deal about the financial world. I had access to the internet all day and could do a lot of my own work on my smartphone. I knew it wasn't a long term career for me, so I saved as much money as possible and spent the last few months carefully planning my escape strategy.

I had at least two hours per day of down time. I used this time to write, read and network with people online. In the last few months after I had decided I no longer wanted to continue working there, I avoided taking on new customers so I could maximize my free time to write this book.

I had the Google Docs app installed on my iPhone, so it looked to others like I was texting. This is a very sneaky way to write books! For me it was the only way, since I worked long hours at the dealership. I encourage you to find jobs that have down time, like car sales, hotel front desk, security, health club or building attendant. If your escape plan involves writing books or reading, these jobs are good to have.

In order to improve your job situation, your focus needs to be on incremental change. Most people want instant improvement, but life usually doesn't work that way. Life works best when you have a plan for yourself and work towards that plan every day, no matter how small a step you take. If you follow through, you'll be ahead of most people since following through with a life plan is quite difficult.

If you dislike your job, identify what exactly you dislike. Then find a different job that is less horrible than your current one. Keep doing this until your job situation is acceptable to you.

If for some reason you have to keep your job due to financial or health insurance reasons, and your boss is absolutely killing your soul, you might consider anonymously sending him/her a box of cow dung from shitsenders.com or an envelope full of glitter from shipyourenemiesglitter.com. If you're scared of those two ideas, maybe confessing your true feelings to postsecret.com might be the right option for you. I have seriously considered sending a box of cow dung to past bosses who were uniquely horrible, but I never did. Time dulled my taste for revenge. I don't encourage most people to act on their feelings of revenge. Doing bad things to others usually results only in more bad things coming to you.

But in certain cases, I think it's necessary to take some sort of action in order to move past the horrible situation. In the case of an overly abusive, psychopathic boss, I think it would be a positive thing if he/she were sent a box of elephant crap in the mail. If large numbers of people are being negatively affected by one person who is particularly abusive, then I think some kind of action is necessary. If this abusive person has a lot of power, then the channels one can realistically take become extremely scarce. In this case, the option of anonymously sending a box of crap to a psychopathic boss is a good one.

Or, if you are really adventurous, write a one paragraph story detailing how badly you're being treated at your job. Then email it to uncrapyourlife@gmail.com and for $25 I'll create a video of your experience. I'll then post this to my YouTube channel in a folder named, "Crappy Job Videos Directed By You". It will be 100% anonymous and no one will know that you provided the material. An example of this is the following script that I made into a video before I quit my job. It was taken directly from my experience working at a car dealership. Watching it allowed me to see just how badly I was being treated. Once I saw myself in the video, I realized I couldn't allow myself to be treated badly anymore. The video gave me courage to leave my job.

Here's the script:

Boss is older, white, male, super-controlling, mean and has brown hair.
Boss: "What are you doing? [*Boss Screams*]: You didn't follow the process again!!!!!"
Me: "Uh, well, I was just trying a different way that I thought worked really well"
Boss: "You're an idiot!"
Me: "Well, uh, um....er, I think there's a misunderstanding about what I'm doing. I mean, and uh, if you.....please don't scream at

me anymore. I mean, it's not a good way to talk to people."
Then the last scene shows my finger knocking down a little cartoon man and the message says, "SAY GOODBYE TO YOUR MASTERS".

Making a video about your bad experience is a way for your voice to be heard. It can be a creative outlet that serves the purpose of releasing internal pressure and allowing yourself to understand just how bad things have gotten. You will probably be surprised how many people around the globe will be able to relate your story. And you will most likely feel some relief your truth is finally out. Your story can make others laugh and feel better about their own crappy job experiences.

If you're serious about quitting your job, you need a plan-your-escape-from-your-job vacation. Give yourself lots of time and comfortable moments to concoct your exit strategy and get paid for it too. This way you'll be really prepared for your transition. You also need to use up your vacation pay before you quit because some employers don't reimburse you for unused vacation.

Instead of going on an expensive trip, I used most of my paid vacation to finish this book and put in place my escape plan. I took a two-day trip with my daughter, then committed myself to writing for the remainder of my time off. I've committed myself to working my ass off now so my future can be filled with more freedom, health and happiness.

When I quit my car sales job, I had $6,500 in the bank. But I started doing temp jobs immediately so my money continued to flow in a positive direction. I didn't want to repeat the same mistakes I made in 2009 when I went completely broke. I've recently become an Uber driver, plus I'm being paid to participate in market research studies by Q & A Focus Suites. I have an entrepreneur mentor who is helping me implement more income-generating projects. These jobs allow me to create a life of optimal health and happiness because I don't have a boss and I'm allowed to sleep in the morning.

The main thing to keep in mind is that crappy jobs pay the bills and keep you alive. Until you have your escape plan solidly created, you're going to need to hold on to your crappy job. But don't get discouraged because many people have escaped successfully. If I succeed, I'm going to tell you how I did it. My current plan for creating my own income is: write books, teach online and in-person classes and give speeches. I'm committed to full transparency about my methods because I'll never forget how crappy it feels to work for half-witted vampires. I feel deep empathy for anyone stuck at a job they hate.

Imagine what the world would be like if we all were living up to our true potential. It would be a very fun place to live. It's my belief humans are not meant to suffer needlessly. But it takes a certain amount of suffering before any big changes come to pass in a person's life. Do you think you have suffered enough and know where you want to go in life? I know I have! Let's go!

EXERCISES

If you dislike your job, what specifically do you dislike about it? What are some possible solutions to the situations you dislike at your job?
Do you feel valued at your job?
Are you attached to the suffering you endure at your job?
Do your feelings of hate for you boss overshadow everything else?
Have you ever created a revenge plan for your boss?
If you absolutely cannot deal with your boss anymore, what is stopping you from leaving your job?
Take Action: If your boss is completely horrible, start looking for another job.

8

MY JOBS DON'T UTILIZE MY TALENTS

I'm one of those people whose job pays the bills and nothing more. I know there are tons of people like me. Even though I tried for years to start creative career, I never succeeded. I think I would make a good art director, videographer or creative consultant but I haven't yet convinced a hiring manager of my skills. Because I never landed an amazingly creative position, I experienced a lack of fulfillment in my 9-5 jobs.

During much of my employment I submitted creative project ideas to my superiors, but they were rarely utilized. After years of submitting my concepts and rarely seeing any implementation of them, I stopped providing ideas. Instead, I started creating my own projects, videos, and writing.

SOLUTION: I CREATED A YOUTUBE CHANNEL WHICH FULFILLS ME PLUS MAKES SOME EXTRA MONEY

I started uploading videos to my YouTube channel, Stellabelle, in 2008, three years after YouTube was founded. Here's one of my best videos, *How To Print On A Marshmallow.*

From 2008 to 2011, my channel remained fairly obscure, only receiving about thirty views per day. Then in the fall of 2011, my views started going way up, to a daily count of three hundred. Around the time my channel reached 50,000 combined video views, I received the verified YouTube Partner status from Google. Once this happened, I began to make money from ad revenue because my videos started receiving thousands of views, not hundreds. I got my first check from YouTube in 2012. I do not advertise my YouTube channel anywhere except on my car, so, the data here explores only organic video views, not paid advertisements.

For me, three years into creating my channel, I almost gave up because I was not getting the number of views that would allow me to become a YouTube Partner. Yet making videos is in my blood, so I continued creating them out of passion alone. Later, in the third year, I finally started seeing the results I craved. That's when my views jumped from thirty per day to three hundred. Many people have asked me what factors are responsible for achieving the YouTube Partner status. From what I know, it varies from person to person. For me, it seemed once my channel reached the combined video views of 50,000 I was accepted into the YouTube Partner Program. Some people reach it much faster than I did. The three things you will need in order to become a verified YouTube Partner are passion, persistence and fearlessness.

My most viewed videos are either entertaining/wacky or in the how-to format. My best advice is to create videos that solve problems lots of people have, but do it in a way that is uniquely yours. A great tool to use to research topics people around the world are interested in is Google Trends. It is an amazing, free online tool that shows you how and when people on the planet search for certain words using Google. Google Trends explains why my video, *How To Make Cake Pops,* got around 170 views per day in the fall of 2011, but dropped to 25 views per day in 2013. The YouTube Analytics data for my video corresponds exactly with the Google Trends data for the cake pop trend. I made my video right before the cake pop trend exploded, so it was a combination of timing and subject choice that resulted in 62,827 views of this video. The reason I made the cake pop video was not because I was aware of Google Trends (I just learned about it this year). I made it because I was curious how to make cake pops after visiting a Starbucks and it turned out a lot of people were also curious. You're probably wondering how much money 63,000 video views brings in. It earned $67.

From 2008 until 2011 I had tried in vain to make a viral video. I made all kinds of weird videos. I made strange art films. I filmed myself making weird faces and noises. I filmed a parrot skateboarding. I even made a few music videos. No one cared. No one was watching my videos. It was three years of disappointing analytics. I gave up for a year and had a baby. But something gnawed at me to continue making videos. I decided to give up my earlier strategy of being "weird" and just make videos for fun or to solve problems. The videos that turned it around for me and enabled me to become a YouTube Partner were *How To Make Cake Pops, DIY: Slides To Digital on a Shoestring Budget* and *How To Write With Both Hands Simultaneously.* Before 2011 I had never made any how-to videos and now these were the ones responsible for making me some money.

Striking it rich on YouTube these days is quite difficult due to the enormous amount of competition, but it's not impossible. I always encourage everyone to go for their dreams, yet I also want to show the reality of the ad revenue numbers. Since 63,000 views results in only $67, your videos need a lot of views before any money will come rolling in. (YouTube deposits money in your account only after your ad revenue has reached $100.)

My YouTube channel currently has a combined video view count of 356,262. Also, recently I learned that YouTube is favoring engagement over click through views. This means that YouTube wants creators to make content that holds viewers' attention and they place a higher value on that type of content. This is fairly new because in the past YouTube was only concerned with the amount of views, not how long people watched your videos. YouTube now wants people to make quality content.

I encourage you to build a YouTube channel as an extension of your passions and interests. If you put enough authentic energy into your videos your channel and audience will grow. The best time to create your YouTube channel is today. There are still a lot of voices absent on YouTube. I encourage you to speak your mind, use your authentic voice and let yourself go. The world is waiting for your unique vision!

EXERCISES

What talents do you have that are not being utilized at your job? If you could make a video without the fear of embarrassment, what would you make?
What ideas have you submitted to your superiors that have not been utilized?
What YouTube video ideas do you have?
Do you know anyone who would help you film, edit or give you feedback on your videos?
Take Action: Make one video today about any topic you wish and upload it to YouTube. Email the link to: uncrapyourlife@gmail.com and I will give you feedback.

9

I WAS TERRIFIED OF PUBLIC SPEAKING

We all have fears holding us back, blocking us from living a full life. Many of us know what our fears are, but don't know what to do to overcome them. The first step in conquering any fear is to correctly identify one. You can choose only one. You have to decide you want to overcome this one fear as if your life depended on it. If you don't make a conscious decision to overcome it you will probably never do so. In the story below I detail how I overcame my fear of public speaking. This was one of the scariest things I've ever attempted to change about myself.

I was terrified of public speaking for as long as I can remember. In eighth grade I had to give a speech to my classmates. Before it was my turn, my hands became clammy, my throat dried up, my head went numb and I got a burning sensation in my brain. I thought I was going to die. I was terrified I would make a fool of myself and everyone would tease me about it forever. I cared deeply what others thought of me and didn't want negative judgement from my peers. I was also scared everyone would be able to tell I was dying inside. After it was over, I vowed never to go through that experience again. I avoided giving speeches from then on.

I suffered my entire life from this fear and I realized if I was going to be successful as an entrepreneur, I would have to get over it. I also realized my fear of public speaking was connected to my perfectionistic tendencies and fear of making a fool of myself. This fear had derailed my short-lived career as an ESL teacher in Japan. When I was twenty-nine, I got a job teaching English at a company called AEON in Japan. Unfortunately, I developed a stress disorder as a result of being terrified of speaking in front of a class.

While standing in front of my classes in Japan, I had the sensation of being trapped in a glass bell-jar with hundreds of eyeballs staring me, dissecting my every flaw. I thought after a while my fear of teaching would go away, but it never did. As a result of my traumatic fears, I lost my appetite, lost twenty-five pounds, and began drinking and smoking heavily. After many months of teaching, I became really ill, temporarily lost my hearing, had to break my teaching contract and return to the U.S. I spent the next year recovering at my parents' house. During my recovery, I spent a lot of time walking in the woods, creating my Wrongland postcard series and writing letters to my friend, Daphne.

I didn't overcome my fear of public speaking after resigning from my teaching position. Instead, I completely ignored it.

Fast forward to 2011. I was now entertaining the idea of becoming an entrepreneur because I hadn't really made any progress on any career path. How can I thrive as an entrepreneur if I can't give a speech? This fear was getting in the way of progress. This fear was keeping me down.

SOLUTION: I OVERCAME MY FEAR OF PUBLIC SPEAKING AT AGE 41

During my 41st year of life, I decided to do something about my fear of public speaking. I was tired of this fear ruling my life. I knew the only way I was going to overcome it was to face it head on. I would have to start giving public speeches.

The first step was to secure a speaking engagement. But where? On what topic? There was an event that I attended in San Diego called *Pecha Kucha* that I really loved. People from all walks of life gave speeches on random, fascinating topics. When I first attended *Pecha Kucha*, I realized I wanted to be up there giving a speech on a fascinating topic. I found a *Pecha Kucha* chapter in Kansas City, where I lived, and I wrote a proposal for a speech topic. I was delighted when I received the email letting me know I was selected as a speaker. I gave a speech about my experience visiting the aftermath of the Joplin, Missouri tornado. I had visited Joplin three days after the multi-vortex tornado decimated it in 2011 and documented it with photos and videos.

The experience of giving this first speech was horrible. Just before I entered the stage, my palms turned into wet sponges and my heart raced uncontrollably. I had decided to film myself so I could observe how terrible my public speaking was. Later when I watched the video, I saw I was so nervous during my speech that my leg spasmodically moved back and forth during the entire thing. It was so embarrassing. I committed myself to not doing that in my next speech. I did several more public speeches and by the time I did my 6th one, I was no longer afraid of the experience. In one year I successfully overcame my fear of public speaking.

The steps I took were:

- I committed myself to overcoming my fear at all costs.
- I planned a concrete action to expose myself to the feared experience.
- I repeated doing the feared experience.
- I recorded myself and learned from seeing my mistakes.

- I forgave myself for not being a perfect person.
- I allowed myself to make mistakes without judging myself harshly.

EXERCISES

Name one fear that has plagued you for most of you life.
How have you attempted to overcome a fear in the past?
Are you tired of letting your fear win?
If you're ready to overcome a fear, what is your plan of action?
Are you ready to allow yourself to make mistakes without judgement?
Take Action: Commit yourself to overcoming one fear this year. Just one.

10

PERFECTIONISM IS MY EVIL MASTER

An insane addiction to perfectionism has destroyed a lot of opportunities. Everyone has some trait preventing them from moving forward in life. My biggest flaw is a two-pronged, self-sabotaging sword: perfectionism on one side and the inability to let go on the other. Both of these weaknesses are based in fear. I'm afraid to finish anything because the thought of creating mediocre work terrifies me. For me, finishing something equals the death of an idea. Finishing a project means that I have given up on it. By not finishing something I have the opportunity to make it more perfect in the future. But deep down I know I never will complete it because I'm unwilling to release it.

I knew I had a problem with perfectionism when I'd write and rewrite a letter over ten times before feeling okay about sending it to someone. When I worked as a production artist I would re-work my projects to death. I knew at the time there was something wrong with me and I was working two hundred percent harder than everyone else around me, but I just couldn't help it. I never felt anything was good enough. Letting go of a project was like death to me. The positive sides of my perfectionism were: I received many raises at my jobs, achieved high scores on tests and made some great art. But in life, perfectionism has been more detrimental than helpful to my personal and professional growth.

Art is another matter entirely. I think being a perfectionist and making art is a good combination. Art is an arena where perfectionists can thrive. There are degrees of perfectionism, of course. The debilitating kind of artist would be the perfectionistic one who doesn't know when to finish a piece of work. This is the sort of artist I am. I combat this issue by setting deadlines and sticking to them. I force myself to finish even though I don't want to.

If I look at the deeper issue going on beneath the surface, I see a low opinion of myself is at the root. For some reason self-doubt consumes me. I cannot see my own value and strengths. I'm the person who just shakes my head with doubt when someone pays me a compliment.

I'm a harsh critic of my own work and the work of others. This trait prevents me from attaining success. Self-sabotage is a big part of my mental life. My mind edits every thought and makes it very difficult for me to accomplish anything significant. My mind is my worst enemy. This trait is something I'm now aware of and managing.

I don't understand the origins of my paralyzing perfectionism. I might be obsessive compulsive or have some other mental illness. Or I might just be an over-thinker, under-doer. Anything is possible. But this year I have become painfully aware of why I'm unable to finish anything. I get upset when I see other people throw their mediocre works into the world and find success. I get upset because I'm jealous they don't obsess over every detail of their work like I do. But being jealous isn't getting me very far.

I'm at a point in life which is crucial to the future. I'm middle-aged, have a five year-old daughter and I'm starting to see the negative impacts of my perfectionism. If I don't figure out a way to overcome my perfectionism I will be miserable and I'll probably die that way. My life literally depends on me overcoming this problem.

SOLUTION: LETTING GO OF ILLUSIONS OF PERFECTION AND RELEASING IDEAS TO THE WORLD

One method I've been employing lately is tricking my brain into thinking my life is about to come to an end. I ask the question, "What have I learned in life that will benefit the most people right now?" This line of thinking forces me to act in the present moment. It wakes up my mind to the reality life will end some day. It could even end today. Like many people, I want my life to matter. I don't want to live a meaningless, forgettable existence impacting no one in the present or future. The great difficulty lies in committing myself 100%. Desire is good, daily commitment is better.

I try to manage perfectionism by removing my ego from the equation. Many of my breakthroughs have occurred once I let go of selfish desires and simply expressed a truth or solved a problem that affected a lot of people without thinking how it would benefit me personally.

The biggest component to overcoming perfectionism is to forgive myself for not being perfect. I'm not as scared of making mistakes as I used to be because I don't allow the mistakes to define my personality. I'm starting to view myself as a student of life instead of an adult who has it together. This shift has had positive effects on my ability to finish projects. Instead of fear, I feel excited about the future.

I made a commitment to myself to release this book in 2015. I'm still scared, but since I've made a commitment, I have to go through with it. I moved back the deadline several times because at each stage of writing, I realized it wasn't good enough. I know it is still not perfect. Many people proofread it and I paid close attention to their feedback which I then implemented. The process of exposing my work to many people is entirely new to me. I'm making it up as I go along. It forced me to grow and be forgiving of my shortcomings. My tendency in the past was to hide my projects and not show them to anyone. Now I know it's not good to hide.

The trick is to find the right people to help you and then restrain your ego when they give you good advice. I'm looking forward to reading reviews of this book and learning from them so my next book can be better.

Repeat this to yourself: I am not perfect. No one is or ever will be.
Does this sentence make you feel a little better about yourself? It helps me a lot.

EXERCISES

Do you have perfectionistic tendencies holding you back from accomplishing goals?
What does your perfectionism prevent you from doing?
What do you wish you could do?
What is the underlying cause of your perfectionism?
Give yourself permission right now to make mistakes and be okay with them.
Take Action: Release one thing to the world via email, snail mail or social media you've been holding onto for a long time.

11

I HAD A BABY WITH A SOCIOPATH

I fucked up. I fucked up really bad in 2009. I had a relationship with a sociopath. Then it gets worse: I got pregnant. How did this happen? Why did it happen? I'm still asking myself these questions six years later.

I began to notice disturbing things about this man (who I will from now on refer to as "Crazy-O") a few months after meeting him, but by then it was too late. I was already pregnant. I was 39 years old. I'm trying to understand why I jumped into a relationship with someone who caused me intense pain and fear. I'm still trying to heal myself of this horrible experience. The truth is my desire to be with a man has disappeared completely. I'm plagued by nightmares even to this day.

The years preceding my relationship with Crazy-O were filled with a lot of isolation. I had been putting off having a relationship for many years. I've always been pretty bad at relationships. They are a lot of work. I tend to just like the beginnings of them, when all the happy chemicals are present in my brain.

For most of my life I carried around a terrifying fear of sexually transmitted diseases which prevented me from having normal sexual relationships. At the time I met Crazy-O I was taking an antidepressant called Paxil. This drug made me happy and removed a lot of unpleasant thoughts. It also removed much of my critical thinking abilities. While on Paxil I remember not feeling any sense of danger. I met people with great ease and experienced life without excessive fear and pain. It was wonderful. I remember seeing colors during this time I'd never seen before. But I also wasn't sleeping much. I remember being so tired I would fall asleep in the middle of the day, in public parks or in my car. I knew this was abnormal but I never mentioned it to my doctor because my brain felt so good. Paxil was the greatest high I'd ever experienced and best of all, it was a legal drug prescribed to me by a doctor.

I got involved with Crazy-O immediately after meeting him, without much conscious thought. While on Paxil, I was glad to be free of my hyper-controlling mind. The drug allowed me to let myself go for the first time in my life. I no longer felt afraid of intimacy or getting pregnant. I felt 100% free from all worries.

We had lots of sex after I made Crazy-O get a full lineup of STD tests. I wasn't on any birth control and I didn't insist he wear a condom like I had made other men do for the past 19 years. In fact I'd never had sex without a condom before. I just let everything go. I'd been entertaining the idea of having a child, since it would be then or never. I was 39. I assumed my chances of getting pregnant would be slim because my periods were becoming less heavy. I figured my reproductive abilities had already started to slow down. But I was wrong. I got pregnant instantly. In a matter of weeks of having regular sex I tested positive. This is the point where my life began to fall apart. Around this time, I began to notice odd, scary things about Crazy-O. The first sign he was severely mentally ill took place three months after I met him.

The first situation unfolded like this: Crazy-O had immediately moved into my apartment when he was first fired from his job (very bad sign). Soon after, I felt stifled so I told him I needed a few days to myself. I spent a couple days enjoying my freedom in my apartment. I was happy to be alone. During this time one of his friends called and I was hoarse, so my voice was low. His friend thought I was a man. He immediately told Crazy-O about it.

When Crazy-O came back, he accused me of cheating and was convinced the reason I wanted some space was because I had another man. The next thing he did was so bizarre, I should have broken up with him right then. During this accusation, he sat down cross-legged and repeated about 60 times: "I know you lie, I know you cheat, just admit it now."

It was terrifying. Each time I tried to tell him I never slept with anyone else and I was really alone, he'd just look at me with hate and start repeating his line again, trance-like. He used a brainwashing technique of repeating the same phrase over and over, and refused to listen to me at all. I wasn't able to convince him I was innocent. In fact, I was innocent and I am not the type of person to lie, so it was he who was guilty. He was the kind of person who lied and cheated, so he was incapable of seeing the good in me. He assumed everyone else lied and cheated. I was a mirror of his broken personality.

From this point on my gut instinct told me I should get as far away from this psycho as possible. There was just one huge problem: I was pregnant with his child. So I suppressed my gut instincts and instead tried to envision our life together. I had real trouble visualizing that life. I knew I needed to be around my support system in order to survive. We decided to go back to my parents house. The plan was for him to find work so I could focus on staying healthy and preparing for our child.

He was unable to find a good job. He wanted to pursue his art, but he wasn't good enough to be financially successful. My hope was sinking as the pressures of needing money started to press upon my shrinking lifeline. Things were about to get a lot worse. I was seven months pregnant when more psychological terror set in.

One night while I was in a deep sleep, Crazy-O appeared over my face, wild-eyed, angry and hysterical. He was screaming into my face, "YOU'RE DOING IT AGAIN. YOU ARE A DEMON AND YOU ARE TRYING TO ATTACK ME PSYCHOLOGICALLY WHILE I'M ASLEEP." I was mortified. I was the one being assaulted while he accused me of assaulting him. It was fucking scary and weird. It was something out of a horror movie. I tried to convince him I was doing no such thing, but it was of no use. He was convinced the "demons inside me" were trying to take possession of his spirit. It was then I realized that he either had schizophrenia or was a sociopath, or a combination of both. No one in their right mind would purposely terrify their pregnant girlfriend for fear the fright might have a negative impact on both the baby and the mother. I learned that sociopaths always blame their victims and make their victims feel guilty. Sociopaths never think there is anything wrong with them and instead always place the blame on others.

This same thing happened again a few weeks later. There were countless things like this I endured. I've blocked out many of them. The mental torture was humiliating. My self-esteem was hacked away, bit by bit. Being pregnant made my situation feel particularly hopeless. Suddenly I found myself able to relate to victims of all kinds.

Near the end of our relationship, during one of his freakouts in which he went into a psychological torture session of me, I decided to film him. During this session, he took on my persona and began to act out how I talked to people. He mocked my depressive episodes and acted out the way I was tired all the time (I was *pregnant!*). Then he pretended to be one of my friends responding to me sympathetically. He jeered and sneered throughout this little play of his. It was sick and hurtful. Not knowing how to respond, I announced that I would be filming him but he didn't acknowledge me in any way. His lack of response made me realize that perhaps he had dissociated from reality. I continued to film him through his entire episode and the camera created a buffer between me and the pain he was stirring up inside. Plus, I wanted to document his insanity in case there were any complications of custody later on. I didn't know what lay in store for my daughter's and my future. But my gut instincts told me to document his psychologically abusive behavior. After his session stopped he never mentioned anything about me filming him. How bizarre that was.

I couldn't watch the video for a long time and I finally begged one of my friends to look at it. I craved an objective opinion. Was it as sick as it felt to me? My friend said yes and she admitted it was a lot like watching a horror film.

After these disturbing experiences I sank into a deep depression. I knew I had made a huge mistake by deciding to mate with this man. I feared that my child would be abnormal because Crazy-O's mother was schizophrenic. But my immediate concern was to get away from Crazy-O. Part of me just wanted the quickest way out of the difficulties ahead. I entertained killing myself or having an abortion or disappearing to live on the streets in Japan. There were many times I envisioned driving my car into a cement wall at high speeds.

But I didn't kill myself or get an abortion. I gave birth to a normal baby. But the problems with Crazy-O continued on. Two days after giving birth to my baby, I woke up in the middle of the night for some reason. There was Crazy-O sitting in front of my computer screen looking at Russian porn while my baby lay in his lap asleep. A tiger rose up inside of me. My anger and disgust for this horrid man rose up into a volcanic explosion. It no longer mattered how badly I was being treated, but there was no way in hell I was going to allow him to abuse my little baby. As he sat there with his porn, I said the words I had been meaning to say since the very beginning: "It's over. Get out of our house right now!"

SOLUTION: I FOUND THE INNER STRENGTH TO CUT OFF

TIES WITH CRAZY-O, GAIN FULL CUSTODY OF MY CHILD AND RAISE HER WITH FAMILY HELP

I took my baby back and woke up my parents. I told them I was kicking out Crazy-O that instant. It was 4:30 in the morning and I drove him to the bus station. I cried all the way there. I wasn't crying for him. I cried for myself. I cried for the future in which I would be doing it all alone. I cried for my baby girl, because I knew she would be growing up without a father. I cried because I knew it was going to suck to be a single mother. But my tears also cleaned out all the emotional abuse I'd endured by this scum. I cried because my dream of finding love and intimacy was smashed. When I returned to our house, I found his purple fish dead in its bowl. I had always felt sorry for the fish because it was in such a small bowl. I was relieved to find it dead so I would not be reminded of him anymore. Death is necessary for new life to emerge.

My daughter's and my survival began to be my number-one priority. Something in me changed once I realized I didn't have to be a victim anymore. It would be difficult going it alone but it would be more difficult if I stayed in a relationship that was killing my soul. The game was finally over. It was time for me to face the reality of single motherhood.

After the break up, depression was my constant companion, but work still needed to get done. I hired a lawyer in order to gain full custody of my child. Crazy-O never showed up in court so he forfeited his parental rights. I don't pursue getting child support because I don't want anything to do with him. Once you start accepting money from the father, he will have rights. I prefer to stay as far away from him and have no contact whatsoever.

Right after I broke up with Crazy-O, I finally learned the truth about his criminal past. Several years ago he had been in jail for beating up his ex-girlfriend, who happened to be pregnant with his child. At the time of our break up, this woman got in contact with me, and I requested she send me the hospital and criminal records. I read all the horrifying documents of his records. The lengthy description of the injuries he inflicted on her was especially disturbing. I had a lot of trouble in my mind after I learned the truth about his violent past. I was plagued by nightmares for years after realizing I was intimate with a **sociopathic, abusive criminal.** I really fucked up bad this time. I've never been so terrified in my entire life.

After I broke off all ties with him, he cyber-stalked me for about a year. He created fake Facebook profiles that contained some connection to my interests. His attempts at creating profiles were pretty pathetic and I could tell after a few minutes of studying they were his. However, I was psychologically traumatized because he continued to make fake profiles to gain access to me. At that time, I was scared to accept anyone's Facebook invitation for fear it would be him. Fear became the dominant emotion coursing through my veins. Fear robbed me of joy. I still struggle with the aftereffects of this.

I continue to heal from this traumatic experience. I'm not yet at a point of understanding what life feels like as an emotionally healthy person. The issue I want to work on in the near future is regaining trust in others. I'll be documenting this journey in future posts or books.

The steps I took to get out of the abusive relationship with Crazy-O were:

1. I accepted the reality I would be raising my child completely alone.
2. I got physically far away from him and have no contact.
3. I began the process of psychological healing.
4. I hired a lawyer, at a cost of $1,500 to gain full custody of my child.
5. I changed my child's last name to be the same as my last name.
6. I created a plan for making more money.
7. I moved back into my parents' house so my daughter would be in a safe, supportive environment.
8. I tried not to let fear ruin my life.

9. I actively worked on methods to decrease fear.
10. I don't pursue getting child support from him.

EXERCISES

When you think about living on a deserted island with your boyfriend/girlfriend, what does it feel like to you?

Do you have a sinking feeling in your stomach when you're with your boyfriend/girlfriend at night?

If your boyfriend/girlfriend is abusive to you, what are the reasons you have not left?

Do you have someone in your life who will not judge you if you tell them what's going on?

If you are in an abusive relationship, write down some steps you need to take to leave him/her.

Ask your friends and family their honest opinion of your boyfriend/girlfriend.

Take Action: Look up the word, *"traumatic bonding"* in Wikipedia

12

MY SEX DRIVE GOT KILLED

I haven't had sex for almost 6 years. Not only have I not done it, I have not thought about it, either. Ok, there were about 6 days in 6 years where I considered having sex with someone. My sexual fantasies have for the most part disappeared. Gone. Zapped. The thought of touching someone in a sexual way is repulsive to me. I have regressed to an immature state. This is definitely tied to my recent experience of being involved with a sociopathic boyfriend. I am most likely still suffering from Post Traumatic Stress Disorder. But there is a positive side to this experience.

SOLUTION: AS A RESULT OF NOT HAVING SEX, I PSYCHOLOGICALLY CLEANSED MYSELF

Because my sexual motives have disappeared, I can talk to any man, even super intelligent, successful or attractive ones, with great ease. It's much like I've turned into a block of wood fashioned into the shape of a human. I've lost all sexual impulse. This is perhaps the most beautiful gift I've ever been given because I am free of suffering. Desiring sex and not getting it is a form of hell. Not desiring it at all is bliss.

Before this, I remember becoming really nervous when an attractive man came near me. My heart would race, my cheeks would become flushed, my stomach would churn. All I could think about was how I was going to "get" him. I became really self-critical and hyper-interested in learning all about a man's personality, everything about him. Men were objects for me to obsess over. I was addicted to the build up of sexual desire and fantasy. My imagination was always over-stimulated by desire, and I developed some obsessive traits for many years. There existed a lot of confusion in my brain when my fantasy of the men I obsessed over, did not occur in reality. I realize now, I never wanted reality. I wanted the fantastical worlds my mind was constantly constructing around desirable objects. I confused sexual desire with art.

Now I'm not attached to the idea of attachment. I no longer feel attachment will be able to dissolve the void buried within my interior. I have come to accept the void within me and I no longer waste energy attempting to find humans to dissolve it. All of my previous attempts to remove this void have failed. I'm left with just one option: to fully embrace and accept the great emptiness. I have come to understand that no one or no thing can fill this for me. It is meant to just be there in its natural dark state.

Jacques Lacan wrote extensively about sexual sublimation:

"Das Ding is the German for 'the thing' though Lacan conceives it as an abstract notion and one of the defining characteristics of the human condition. Broadly speaking it is the vacuum one experiences as a human being and which one endeavours to fill with differing human relationships, objects and experiences all of which serve to plug a gap in one's psychical needs. For this reason Lacan also considers Das Ding to be a non-Thing or vacuole.[16] The relationships which one relies on to overcome the vacuity of Das Ding are always insufficient in wholly satisfying the individual."

I am lucky to have constant access to the creative ideas burning inside my brain these days. Sexual attachment, for me, does not have an enhancing effect upon the fruition of ideas. It has the effect of diluting my purest thought energy and warping it's direction. Therefore, abstaining from sexual urges is in my best interest since my number one priority is caring for and developing my creative projects. Sexual sublimation is having an almost mystical (I don't like the word, *mystical,* but in this respect, it fits) effect upon my brain. I have strong visions daily which I then put into action. There were many years when I lost my ability to create and act upon pure creative impulses. But my ability is back. I'm grateful I became involved with a man who destroyed my trust in the male species. I've been reunited with my imagination because of that disaster. I feel lucky. Maybe I'm deluded, maybe not. I'll know in time.

Too much emphasis in our culture is placed on sex. When people hear that I haven't had sex in six years, they generally respond with, "Oh, you poor little thing. That's awful." What people don't realize is, losing my sex drive was perhaps the best thing ever to have happened to me. My feelings of crazy lust are mostly gone and my thoughts and actions are now based in more pure motives, like improving my daughter's life and our financial future. I'm still human, of course, and occasionally I am gripped with a mad desire for someone who lies out of my reach, but I view these feelings as a normal part of life. Also, I'm open to the possibility in the future, my sexual feelings will return. I'm not placing any rules on my life. Instead, I'm releasing myself to the natural flow of life. I'm paying attention to self-care and I'm following through with creative projects. I think in abstaining from sex I've been forced to confront and overcome my own weaknesses. I'm a stronger, more sane person now.

EXERCISES

What are the reasons you lost your sex drive?
Do you want your sex drive back or are you happy without it?
What is something you have gained while your sex drive was absent?
What do others think about your sex drive?
How do you feel about your sex drive?
Take Action: Write about your sex drive, even if it's just for yourself.

13

I WANTED TO DIE

I've had many low points in my life. I have a natural tendency to spiral inwards, so I've entertained thoughts of killing myself many times during my low points. There's lots of suicide on both sides of my family, so maybe it's a genetic predisposition. Two of my cousins killed themselves and my father attempted suicide about twenty years ago. Thankfully, my dad received treatment and is doing well now. I'm very grateful he survived his life-threatening depression and is healthy today.

My most recent low point was by far the lowest point in my life and I seriously entertained killing myself on and off for several months. I never did act on these thoughts, but thinking about suicide relieved some of the pressure I was feeling.

When I was in a relationship with Crazy-O, I had severe trouble seeing how I would ever be free of him. I was pregnant with his baby and I felt trapped! I thought being pregnant meant that I would never be free of him. After being with him for six months,

I knew Crazy-O was an emotionally damaged person. I knew he lacked empathy and would further damage both me and my child. I knew I had a made a terrible mistake by getting involved with him. I couldn't visualize how to to get away from him and I wasn't yet able to embrace the idea of raising a baby by myself. I didn't know the steps I needed to take in order to raise a baby on my own. There were too many steps! There was too much fear associated with each step so my mind just added up all the fearful steps and decided it was too much to handle. I did not acknowledge these gut instincts and instead tried to continue the relationship with Crazy-O.

Then thoughts of death began to creep in. Death seemed like the easiest way out. I visualized driving myself over a bridge or into a cement wall. I imagined running in front of a train. I thought of various ways to acquire morphine or heroin. I thought it would be a good idea to have several methods of suicide going at once. So, I could overdose on heroin then jump off a bridge. In this way, death would be guaranteed.

But there was one big problem: I had a baby inside me! I couldn't kill myself with a baby growing inside of me. I considered abortion. Abortion would solve the big problem of needing to get away from Crazy-O and sever the ties between us. I seriously considered getting an abortion for a few days. Ah, but I felt that I would regret an abortion too much. I realized this was most likely the last and only chance of having a baby. I decided to grit my teeth, break up with Crazy-O, have a baby and find out how to survive in the world of single motherhood. I decided not to kill myself even though I wanted to. It's been hell but I'm glad I decided to have a baby. My daughter is a great source of inspiration to my life. But I'll never get pregnant by a crazy man again. Being pregnant almost killed me.

SOLUTION: I STARTED BELIEVING IN MYSELF AND TAKING ACTION

Now instead of wishing I was dead, I wish for other things. But I work more than I wish. I spend time trying to finish projects and I dream of future events. I try new things and am okay with failure. I'm starting to get some good feelings back. I'm still feeling a lot of numbness but I can at least envision a future bright and full of wonder. I'm beginning to feel that it's within my reach again. I'm beginning to feel I deserve it.

So how did I start believing in myself? To break through my wall of self-hate and self-criticism, I acknowledged I have been through some shit. I took in deep breaths and felt grateful I managed to escape from a life of hell with my ex-boyfriend. I compared my current mental state with the one I had when I was with him. I now feel a sense of freedom in my present life. Every time I see my daughter smile, I feel happy knowing I saved her from being emotionally damaged.

The day I started to believe in myself was the day I told Crazy-O to get out of my house. Up until that day I always felt squeamish when I told someone, "No." I spent my entire life saying "Yes" even when my heart was feeling "No." I was a doormat. Believing in myself began with standing up for myself and telling him, "No."

Another way I believe in myself is allowing myself to fail. I now view mistakes as lessons. I stay strong and I don't let the mistakes drag me into a black hole of doom. I have a tendency to ruminate and dissect my mistakes in order to figure out root causes and possible future solutions. This tendency also occasionally thrusts me into depressive ruts. I have to remain vigilant about this personality trait and force myself out of the black hole once I find myself in it.

I'm no longer afraid of failure because my past relationship defined failure in every way. Hey, I'm still alive despite wanting to kill myself! That is a success. The fact my child is happy and healthy is an indicator that I've done some things right.

I no longer think about death or killing myself. Those thoughts emerged because I did not pay attention to my gut instincts and found myself in a dangerous situation with a dangerous person.

Those thoughts acted as a warning system that my life was in serious danger and I needed help.

From that failed relationship these lessons have emerged:

- Say "No" when my heart feels "No".
- Recognize when someone is abusing me.
- Don't trust strangers even if they're charismatic.
- Always seek social proof of someone before you start dating him/her.
- Understand all people have a dark side.
- Forgive myself when I make mistakes.
- Set boundaries and let people into my life slowly.
- Get to know someone inside and out before having sex.

EXERCISES

Do you feel your future is full of possibilities or not?
Do you sometimes feel like you want to die in order to solve a problem?
Do believe you can change your life?
Do you forgive yourself when you make a mistake?
Are you suffering in a situation that feels overwhelming?
Take Action: If you really feel like you want to die, call this number to just talk to someone:
1 (800) 273-8255. I've called them before when I felt really shitty.

14

MY EXCUSE FOR BEING A LOSER: "I DON'T HAVE ENOUGH TIME"

Working a full-time job and taking care of a young child doesn't leave a lot of time for cultivation of entrepreneurial ideas. An average weekday for me goes like this: I wake up my daughter, get her ready for school, get myself ready, walk her to the bus, work from 9 am to 7 pm, then make dinner when I get home, go on Facebook, check email, get her ready for bed, read to her, then go to bed. Sometimes, I just can't do it all and my mother gets my daughter ready for school. I have a short fuse in the morning and I notice I get angry easily. My intense reaction to stress is the real issue that I'm actively working on deconstructing.

My free time consists of tiny moments during the weekdays and bigger chunks of time on the weekends. Instead of socializing, I spend my time writing, making art or doing social media. I feel like I don't have enough time to really pursue getting feedback for my entrepreneurial ideas. Sometimes this lack of time makes me depressed. It makes me feel like I'll never get ahead and will always be poor. I often tell myself, "I don't have enough time to truly change my circumstances."

Six months ago, I did not believe I had enough free time to complete this book. I still struggle with thinking I don't have enough time to do my projects. I recall many months ago a writer friend gave me this advice, "Just write several hundred words every day or when you have time. You'll be able to complete your book easily." I didn't believe her. I told her I didn't have enough time to write a book. I created excuses. I felt defeated.

SOLUTION: I CARVED OUT TIME FOR WRITING AND REDUCED FACEBOOK TIME

That conversation forced me to examine my free time activities. I spent most of my free time on social media. Why? For starters, I rarely leave my house except to go to work. Social media is my substitute for a social life. What did Facebook do for me? What was Facebook doing to my brain? It was obviously triggering something in my brain, but what? I wasn't using it for romantic purposes. I was using it as my main form of communication with people who are trying to change their life, like me. I was also using it to get a reaction from people in order to feel alive. Sometimes I just feel dead inside and going on social media helps my brain feel stimulated. There aren't many people in my vicinity whom I feel closely connected to, so social media is the place I go to get those feelings of connectedness and positive brain chemicals.

I also felt I didn't have enough time to accomplish anything significant on my work days, so I went on social media to make use of what little free time I felt I had. I hopped on Facebook instead of writing one or two paragraphs. I hopped on Facebook to numb myself to the reality that writing a book would take months of intense focus and work. I went on social media to calm my nerves also.

So, a few months ago, I decided to replace my Facebook habit with a writing habit. I tricked my brain and it worked. Every time my brain said, "I'd like to go on Facebook now," I told my brain, "Ok, now you're going to write". So I wrote. At first, my brain wasn't very happy because it wasn't getting rewarded with social media notifications, which Tim Ferriss refers to as *cocaine pellet dispensers*. My brain only got frustration feedback in the beginning because writing is a form of deep thinking and my mind was pretty scrambled. My writing was disjointed, repetitive, messy and contained bad grammar. No wonder no one follows through and finishes a book! It's very frustrating. After a while, though, writing helped my brain think more clearly and deeply. It became a source of happiness and therapy.

It's important to replace your bad habit with a desirable new habit instead of trying to get rid of it. Your bad habit is providing something nourishing for your brain so you must first understand what this habit is giving you. If you're addicted to social media, you have to understand what specifically you're getting out of it. Is it a substitute for face-to-face contact or do you rely on it to boost your self-esteem?

For me, I have a lot of creativity churning inside my brain, so I need to create outlets that are stimulating to both my brain and bank account. Spending huge amounts of time on Facebook is not creating abundance in my bank account. When I go on Facebook now, I am more focused on my writing business and I make sure to thank people when they comment on my professional page. Creating a new habit is very hard work and takes months of conscious effort. It's also painful. But you can do it. You wouldn't be reading this book if you didn't want to change your life in some way.

I said this to myself every time I wanted to give up on this book:

"I must finish it not because I think it's going to be great, but because I need to prove to myself I am capable of finishing something."

EXERCISES

Do a thorough, objective analysis of your free time activities.
How much free time do you have each week?
Are you avoiding completing your own projects?
If you're avoiding completing your own projects, what excuse are you using?
Has social media completely replaced your social life?
If you've noticed you spend too much time on social media, what does social media do for your brain?
Take Action: Become aware of what you're doing in your free time. If you don't like what you're doing, replace one thing you dislike with one new thing that enhances your life.

15

THE BEAUTIFUL RESULTS OF UN-CRAPPING MY LIFE SO FAR

Since I began the sincere quest to un-crap my life, I've noticed some amazing results. My health is improving. I once again am blessed with creative visions. I'm taking great risks by admitting super personal truths and am creating actions that are based in hope, health and possibilities.

I began driving for Uber recently and this experience has greatly improved my sense of mental well-being because I no longer have a crappy boss. I'm not going to get rich driving for Uber, but I view this job as a way to make fast cash and meet fun people. Many of the people I meet are genuinely interested in finding out more about me and this book. I have my book title advertised on the side of my car in magnetic letters and I've decided to just keep the letters there. This way, I'm making money and advertising my book at the same time.

The other fantastic thing is the aches and pains in my feet, joints and back have nearly disappeared. I think the constant intense stress from my job was making me sick. I haven't felt this good in many years, and I'm delighted to discover good health may still be within reach. Now that my pain is disappearing, I can start to enjoy healthy activities, like swimming again. I'm still working on figuring out ways for my body to reduce cortisol production. After years of work stress and negativity, my body still is producing too much cortisol.

Probably the absolute best thing is my imagination has returned in full force. I had lost touch with it during the last few years, mainly because I was emotionally damaged plus I had a job I hated. But now that I have removed the crappy job blockage and am in therapy, my idea flow and innate creativity have returned and show no signs of slowing down. So, what things have I done so far? Here's a list:

1. I drew a whimsical picture of James Altucher and sent it to him in the mail.

After receiving my drawing, James sent me a direct message: "Leah, what a beautiful picture. Thank you. I am going to frame it. It's really special and I appreciate you taking the time to do it. You are a real talent." He then accepted my Facebook friend request. Claudia Azula Altucher has also become my Facebook friend and I appreciate her kindness, creativity and responsiveness. My life changed in a profound way on the day I sent out the drawing to James Altucher. I didn't send it out right away. I let it sit on a bookshelf for over a month. As I glanced up at it one day during a particularly boring moment, I just decided to send it out without thinking too much about it or what would happen as a result. I had become detached. Passion first, and when you are ready to formulate actions, you need to possess a large dose of detachment. My drawing was sincere and heartfelt and I think James could sense this.

2. I sent a proposal to Tesla Motors.

My proposal contained a list of 20 reasons Tesla Motors should lease me a Tesla for free while I'm an Uber driver. The idea emerged while speaking to one of my Uber customers about how cool Tesla Motors is. The idea emerged because I thought it would be a great way for people to be introduced to electric vehicles. I haven't received a response from Tesla Motors. However, the important thing was, I did not let my vision of sending a proposal to Elon Musk be dismissed in my mind. I did not let fear of being perceived as a nutjob stand in the way of following through with my vision. The proposal was created out of a passionate desire to help Tesla Motors become accepted and embraced by the mainstream. The other reason, I'm not going to deny, is because I desire to own a Tesla right now. Not in three years, or five, but now, right now. I am not in a financial position to own a Tesla at this moment, but I'm planning to own one eventually. My proposal would solve a myriad of problems, and that is why I felt compelled to send it. Thinking more deeply about my proposal made me realize there was a significant selfish component in it. The existence of this selfish component has downgraded my opinion of it, and therefore, I will not be disappointed if it's denied by Tesla Motors. The lesson I learned by sending the proposal is, I need to come up with less selfish proposals in the future. I think perhaps this was the true lesson.

3. I joined the Choose Yourself Facebook group.

Choose Yourself is the title of a book written by James Altucher. The philosophy is essentially this: you cannot wait for anyone to bestow importance or power upon you. When you choose yourself, you stop being a victim. When you choose yourself, you free yourself. This philosophy resonated with me at the right moment in life, when I was becoming aware of the many craptraps preventing me from creating a life I wanted to live.

The Choose Yourself Facebook group was formed by one of James Altucher and Claudia Azula Altucher's passionate and driven fans, Georgie-Ann Getton. Within two months of joining this group it has become a very useful resource for my predicament. The people in this group are all wanting to make big changes in their lives. There are writers, nurses, entrepreneurs, office workers, the unemployed, artists, computer programmers, retired people, alcoholics and the list goes on. The most common theme of the group is: moving towards true passion and away from a life of drudgery.

A Choose Yourself member gave me advice I still carry with me every day I work on this book. One day I posted a question, "What if my first book sucks?" He answered, "Everyone's first book sucks. Then you write your second and third one. They will suck less." His response ripped apart my perfectionist crutch and replaced it with a seed of possibility.

We are all at different stages of growth in the group. We all have different skills and try to help each other by giving encouragement or suggestions. This group is precious to me because I have limited contact with people in real life who can give me constructive criticism and support for my entrepreneurial ideas. I simply do not have enough free time. This group is unlike any other Facebook group I've ever joined because people actually provide support, encouragement and new ideas. And in return, I like to give people suggestions in the area of making videos and trying out adventurous marketing ideas. It feels really great to help someone take the first step into an area they are unfamiliar with. I've made a lot of new friends who are in similar situations and they support me. Finding a group like this has been a big reason why I feel I can move forward with my entrepreneurial plans. I recommend it highly to anyone who is thinking about making a serious move towards living out dreams. This group has made Facebook a pleasurable place again. Best of all, it's a closed group so I can really let myself go and admit embarrassing truths.

When you realize you are the only architect of your personal craptrap, you will figure out how to dismantle it, brick by brick. Say this to yourself, "I created this crappy situation. I can take the necessary steps to remove the crap and replace it with something better." You may need to borrow someone else's glasses in order to see how extensive and intricate your craptrap is. This happened to me when I found the Choose Yourself community. Every time I thought about my friends in the CY group, I began to view my self-made craptraps through their lenses. I felt embarrassed that I was being disrespected every day at my job. Their support, caring and advice began to shape the way I un-crapped various aspects of my life. But without a personal commitment to un-crapping my life, their supportive words would not have impacted me in a significant way. I was and still am determined to create a life I love. I'm determined to un-crap my life.

EXERCISES

What entrepreneurial ideas do you have?
Do you know people who are willing to give you feedback for your ideas?
What do you do well?
Could you benefit from a helpful group of people?
What are your main constraints in life right now?
Take Action: Check out the Choose Yourself Facebook page and open your mind to possibilities.

EPILOGUE

In attempting to write an epilogue for this book, I regret to inform you that my inner negativity whore decided to take over my brain. I struggled for almost a month trying to write an earth-shattering conclusion. I got psychologically crushed by the pressure. Paralyzed!

I posted my predicament in the Choose Yourself Facebook group:

> "I'm struggling with writing a conclusion because I've fallen back into my own craptrap! My mind has really become a negativity whore!"

A Choose Yourself member, Katie Ulrych, responded:

> "LOL. My mind becomes a negativity whore too when I try to finish something. I like the term *negativity whore*. Maybe that's how you should end it. By admitting your negativity whore has come out and so it's time to be finished. I love when people admit that kind of stuff. It makes them more human."

And so I'm ending it now. I hope my negativity whore leaves my brain soon. Before she gets any crazy ideas like changing the locks on all the doors in my brain, I'm getting this book self-published!

It is my sincere hope you have learned a new tool or method for un-crapping your life. If your life doesn't need to be significantly un-crapped, then I hope you have at least been entertained.

Send questions or comments to uncrapyourlife@gmail.com

SURPRISE GEMS

Congratulations! You've made it to the hidden gems! Thank you so much for buying my book. You've helped me un-crap my life.

Now that you've made it to the end of my book, I'm interested in finding out what part of your own life you'd like to un-crap. Send an email to uncrapyourlife@gmail.com and in one paragraph, explain the craptrap you're currently in. I will then create one digital art piece which will express your situation and/or help you to visualize a solution. *I'm doing this for the first 25 emails I receive.* I'll email it back to you. The digital art will be yours to do whatever you want with. You can print, reprint, make postcards, reproduce, or make a million dollars. As long as you give me credit, I'm fine.

Let me know if you want your digital art piece to be private or public. If you choose public then I'll require that you give your consent for me to use the digital art in whatever way I want. If you choose private, then I will not share it publicly. It will remain a secret between you and me. The purpose of making the digital art is to thank you and inspire you to un-crap some aspect of your life. By sharing it publicly, you might inspire others to do the same.

This digital art is my gift to you for purchasing my book. I'm planning on doing many more creative gratitude projects in my future books.

Un-crap your life before it's too late!

Sincere Thanks,

Stellabelle

ABOUT THE AUTHOR

Stellabelle doesn't promise you the universe. But she'll help you peel back the layers of your confusing life and hand you an oxygen mask when you start to faint. What separates Stellabelle from other writers is her ability to dissect miserable situations and create interesting solutions that anyone can implement. She can help you start something new or escape from your own hell.

Stellabelle is an artist, writer and YouTuber. She views life as a giant experiment. She likes to swim. She loves nature, technology, electric cars and creating new things. She loves spending time with her family.

This is her first book. She received a B. A. in East Asian Studies from the University of Kansas. She has lived in Kansas City, Chicago, Tucson, Tokyo, Sasebo and San Diego.

Join her email newsletter to be notified about her upcoming books and other cool stuff:
http://leahstephens.weebly.com/sign-up-for-my-newsletter.html

Connect with Stellabelle on social media:

Personal Blog: http://leahstephens.weebly.com/
Twitter: https://twitter.com/stellabelle
Instagram: https://instagram.com/gostellabelle
YouTube: https://www.youtube.com/user/stellabelle

ABOUT THE AUTHOR

FB Page: https://www.facebook.com/youtubestellabelle
Medium: https://medium.com/@stellabelle
Pinterest: https://www.pinterest.com/gostellabelle/
LinkedIn: https://www.linkedin.com/in/stellabelle

ACKNOWLEDGEMENTS

Thanks to my mother and father for their unwavering love for my daughter and belief in me. Also, thanks to my brother Scott and his wife Lilia for their financial support.

Thanks goes to Rachel Ellyn and Dennis Young for editing every line.

Thanks to my editor David Conrads, Michele The Trainer, Elizabeth Allen, Daphne Young, Michael Paine, Carole Ann Borges, Claudia Azula Altucher and the Choose Yourself community.

And a special thanks goes to Sertaç Yakin from the Choose Yourself Facebook community. He recently wrote something which resonates with the theme of this book:

> "I found a table which receives an amazing morning sun light. It's good to feel the warmth. Reading the book for the second time. This time with notes. I know I'll make it. I know I will succeed. And create bunch of abundance. This time or the next or the next. Because I have to get out this vicious cycle. Where people hurt each other for money. Hurt me for money. Fuck anyone who hurts me. Sun feels good. Especially when you are tired and you have a back pain. And you are recovering."

32467055R00058

Made in the USA
San Bernardino, CA
06 April 2016